HEATHROW IN PHOTOGRAPHS

CELEBRATING 75 YEARS OF LONDON'S AIRPORT

Sunsets from the top of the 87m-high control tower can be quite spectacular. (NATS photograph)

HEATHROW IN PHOTOGRAPHS

CELEBRATING 75 YEARS OF LONDON'S AIRPORT

ADRIAN M. BALCH

The
History
Press

Cover illustrations: Front, clockwise from top left: The original control tower at London Airport North when the airport opened in 1946 (Graham Bridges collection); The scene today as a Singapore Airlines Airbus A380 lifts off from Runway 27L (Author); A spectacular view from the current control tower (NATS photograph); BEA Tridents on stand on 3 July 1968 (Tom Singfield collection).
Back: Livery change for British Airways seen on 19 May 1986, with the tail of Boeing 747-136, G-BBPU, in Landor colours framing a Lockheed TriStar still in Negus colours (Author).

First published 2016, this paperback edition published 2021

The History Press
97 St George's Place
Cheltenham, Gloucestershire, GL50 3QB
www.thehistorypress.co.uk

© Adrian M. Balch, 2016, 2021

The right of Adrian M. Balch to be identified as the Author of this work has been asserted in accordance with the Copyright, Designs and Patents Act 1988.

British Library Cataloguing in Publication Data.
A catalogue record for this book is available from the British Library.

ISBN 978 0 7509 9675 4
Typesetting and origination by The History Press
Printed in Turkey by Imak

CONTENTS

INTRODUCTION

Having grown up in the 1950s and '60s, aviation has been a big part of my life and an enthusiasm for it has stayed with me ever since I was young. Witnessing the changes in air transport and technology has been fascinating and amazing, and nowhere more so than at London Heathrow Airport which I visited for the first time in the early 1960s. As Heathrow celebrates its 75th Anniversary in May 2021, this book is an unashamed celebration of that airport, the airliners and memorabilia, photographs of which I hope you will enjoy and maybe even relate to, whatever your age.

Adrian M. Balch

↑This guidebook was published in 1954 and was printed in preparation for the opening of the new Central Area and also BEA's first Vickers Viscounts.

ACKNOWLEDGEMENTS

Special thanks should go to the following people who contributed photographs: Graham Bridges, Ian Haskell, Richard Vandervord, Steve Bond, Paul Burge, Tom Singfield, John Hughes, Pete Bish, Rachael Fraser/NATS (National Air Traffic Services) and Richard Andrews.

All photographs were taken by the author or from the author's collection, unless otherwise credited. In each case, every attempt has been made to identify the original photographer, but if there are any omissions please accept my apologies.

ONE

THE EARLY DAYS

Hailed as the world's busiest airport, Heathrow has been a Mecca for aviation enthusiasts for nearly seven decades, and it is celebrating its 75th anniversary of the official opening on 28 May 2021. Before 1930, however, Heathrow was a hamlet – an isolated row of cottages on Hounslow Heath called Heath Row, approximately where Terminal 3 is now.

The history of Heathrow as an airfield can be traced back to 1929 and the Fairey Aviation Company's Great West Aerodrome. On a grass site, now buried beneath the eastern apron, experimental and test flying was carried out during the 1930s, whilst Croydon was London's main airport at the time. During the Battle of Britain, Heathrow became a satellite airfield for Northolt and operated Hurricane fighters. In the following years, RAF Transport Command and the Air Ministry started looking for sites close to London suitable for long-range transport operations. In 1942, a survey of possible sites was begun and the area immediately north-east of Stanwell was chosen due to ideal building conditions, good communications, room for future expansion and low local population density.

Work commenced on the new airfield in June 1944, but the war ended before the initial runway triangle could be completed and it became necessary to reconsider the future development of the airfield in the light of new civil requirements. It was decided to establish Heathrow as London's primary airport and expansion work continued on land originally acquired by the vicar of Harmondsworth. The new airport was built by Wimpey Construction and the work enlarged the pre-war airfield, demolishing Heathrow hamlet in the process to make room for it. The RAF never got to use the airport.

TWO

1946 – THE AIRPORT OPENS

On 1 January 1946 control of the new airport was formally handed over to the Ministry of Civil Aviation. The first flight departed on that day in the form of Avro Lancastrian *Star Light* of British South American Airways on a route-proving flight to Buenos Aires, via Lisbon for refuelling.

↙Entrance to London Airport North from the car park of the Bricklayers Arms, 1946. (Graham Bridges collection)

↓London Airport North in May 1946, with tents for terminal buildings. (Graham Bridges collection)

↑Inside one of the terminal tents in 1946, comfortable armchairs and flowers try to distract from the conditions. (Graham Bridges collection)

↑The original control tower at London Airport North in the late 1940s. (Graham Bridges collection)

→On 1 January 1946 the first airliner to depart London Airport was Avro Lancastrian G-AGWG *Star Light* of British South American Airways, flown by Don Bennett and R. Clifford Alabaster on a proving flight to South America. The first commercial flight followed ten weeks later. (Graham Bridges collection)

←The movements board is updated by hand on 2 September 1948. (Via Tom Singfield)

↓Early plane spotters in the viewing enclosure c.1949, with a Trans-Canada Airlines Canadair North Star in the background. (Via Tom Singfield)

Heathrow Airport was officially opened by the then minister of Civil Aviation, Lord Winster, on a very wet Thursday 31 May 1946 as 'London Airport', with just the single runway. With a new control tower, but only tents for terminal buildings, London's main airport relocated from Croydon with a view to expansion, but in those early years little could have presaged the huge metropolis that is today's London Heathrow.

On the afternoon of Heathrow's opening ceremony, the first arrivals were two direct services from New York's La Guardia Airport. A Pan American Airways (Pan Am) Lockheed Constellation brought in Robert L. Cummings, the manager of Pan Am's Atlantic Division, followed by another Constellation of American Overseas Airline, carrying the company vice president and general manager, Hal R. Harris. The first fare-paying passenger departed two days later on 28 May 1946 aboard British Overseas Airways Corporation (BOAC) Lancastrian G-AGLS, bound for Australia, the route of which was jointly shared with QANTAS.

↖A view from London Airport North *c.*1951, with the new Central Area control tower visible in the distance. (Via Tom Singfield)

↑1949 and BOAC Avro Lancastrian G-AGLY *Norfolk* about to depart with a BOAC Avro York behind.

←A Pan American World Airways Lockheed Constellation brings in Robert L. Cummings, the manager of Pan Am's Atlantic Division on the afternoon of Heathrow's opening ceremony, 31 May 1946.

The high winds and driving rain that week were not really appropriate for the terminal facilities of those days, which comprised a number of large tents with floors of clinker and sand covered with coconut matting to soak up the water! Permanent buildings had yet to be built and office accommodation for the airlines was provided in caravans. The only brick building was the former RAF north side control tower.

Right from the start, aviation enthusiasts started to gather, mingling with well-wishers waving to the aircraft coming and going. It was clear that the public were very keen on aviation and the airport was keen to promote the aircraft and aviation in the UK. It was quite easy for anyone to walk out across the taxiway during those early days, so a wooden staked fence was erected as a viewing area and chairs were made available. The Green Dragon Café was a regular haunt for enthusiasts to brag about the latest 'Connie' or 'Strat' they had copped! Pleasure flights were arranged using

←An aerial view of the airport in 1949, showing construction of the runway layout and Central Area under way.

↑One of the first official London Airport guidebooks, c.1953 priced 1s.

→ Two adverts that appeared in the first guidebook.

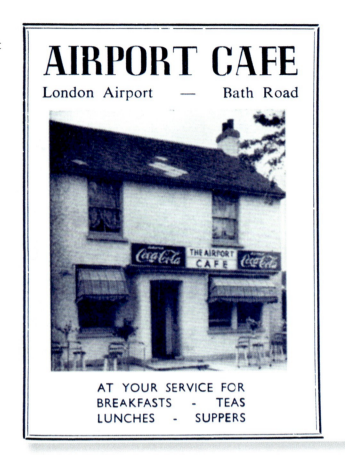

AIRPORT CAFE

London Airport — Bath Road

AT YOUR SERVICE FOR
BREAKFASTS - TEAS
LUNCHES - SUPPERS

The Epicurean Viscount

Best French luncheon on best British Turbo-prop

LONDON–PARIS
daily

Air France

Air France, 52 Haymarket, S.W.1

a pair of Dragon Rapides operated by Island Air Services to promote air travel and to see the new airport from the air, and special coach tours were available to tour the new airport.

By the beginning of 1947, the full expansion plans for the airport's future development were known. They included a pattern of three sets of parallel runways – nine in all, enabling take-offs and landings to be made in any direction subject to the prevailing wind conditions – and a Central Area within the runway pattern for the permanent terminal buildings and three maintenance areas to the east, south-east and south-west of the runways. Plans to extend to the north were abandoned finalising the area within 2,827 acres. With the new central area now surrounded by runways, the only way for access was to build a tunnel beneath the runway on the northern side of the airport, basically linking London Airport North with the Central Terminal Area. A deep trench over 2,000ft long was therefore dug, within which a reinforced concrete shell 2,060ft long, 86ft wide and 23ft high was constructed, subdivided internally to provide inbound and outbound pedestrian paths and cycle tracks, flanking inbound and outbound dual vehicular carriageways. This tunnel is still in use today.

Meanwhile, development of two of the three maintenance areas had been proceeding steadily, the largest of which had been allocated to BOAC. Between 1947 and 1950, eight temporary steel hangars, each of about 100ft span, were constructed for a large part of BOAC's major aircraft maintenance. However, with the possibility of an expanding fleet of larger airliners, it was soon apparent that a larger structure would eventually have to replace these hangars and it would need an unobstructed entrance far in excess of 100ft.

↑BOAC Douglas DC-3, G-AGNG, gets airborne in 1952, with the new Central Area control tower under construction just visible in the distance.

→A memorial statue to Alcock & Brown, who pioneered the first non-stop transatlantic flight in a Vickers Vimy in 1919, was erected on site in 1954 and is seen here being passed by Pan Am Stratocruiser N1036V on 6 December 1954, inbound from New York.

SIR JOHN ALCOCK
AND
SIR ARTHUR WHITTEN BROWN
WHO MADE
THE FIRST DIRECT FLIGHT ACROSS THE ATLANTIC
VICKERS VIMY AIRCRAFT · ROLLS ROYCE ENGINES
ST. JOHN'S NEWFOUNDLAND · CLIFDEN, IRELAND
14TH TO 15TH JUNE 1919

↑A Pan Am crew checks out Boeing Stratocruiser N1029V *Clipper Golden Eagle* prior to departure in 1954. During the early 1950s, Pan Am and American Overseas Airlines operated Statocruisers into London Airport in direct competition on the North Atlantic route operated by BOAC. (Author's collection)

↗Early television sets being loaded aboard BOAC Boeing Stratocruiser G-AKGH *Caledonia* at London Airport North in 1955. (BOAC photograph)

→A classic period shot: BOAC Stratocruiser G-AKGI *Caribou* seen outside the London Airport North terminal building beneath the tail of BOAC L-749 Constellation G-AHEL in 1955. (BOAC photograph)

THREE

THE 1950S BRING MORE EXPANSION

Northolt had been the home for the newly founded British European Airways (BEA) and Blackbushe was the home of Eagle Airways and other fledgling independent carriers during the early days, but it was not until 1951 that the annual number of passengers handled at Heathrow passed those of Northolt at 796,000 passengers per year. During 1951, there were nearly 280,000 visitors to the public enclosure, to view a total of 49,000 aircraft movements. The public enclosure opened daily from 11 a.m. until dusk, and visitors were frequently seen straining to watch the aircraft in failing

↖BOAC Handley Page HP.81 Hermes 4 *Hannibal* is seen departing in July 1950. (Flight photograph)

↓In 1950 a permanent concrete terminal building was built to replace the tents previously used at London Airport North and is seen still in use for charter and cargo flights in this 1959 view. (Via Graham Bridges)

←Inside the new London Airport North terminal building, here is the BOAC check-in desk in 1954, just before the move to the Central Area. (Graham Bridges collection)

↓A rare colour photograph of BOAC Avro York *Marston* parked outside the BOAC hangars at London Airport North in 1956.

light until closing time, such was their enthusiasm. Admission charges were Adults 6d, children 3d, with parking for cars 1s 6d, motorcycles 6d, bicycles 3d and coaches 5s. In 1953, one million passengers were handled at Heathrow, with Northolt still handling 722,000 passengers in the same year.

In the early days there were still planks across the mud for passengers to enter the tents and huts, but it would not be long before something bigger, better and more permanent was on the horizon. Airlines were keen to get themselves established at the new London Airport and soon, Pan Am was operating Boeing Stratocruisers, Constellations and DC-6s & 7s into London alongside Trans World Airlines (TWA) with their Constellations. Among the first airlines to serve the new London Airport were Air India and Pakistan International with their Constellations, whilst Air France operated the unique Sud Languedoc four-piston-engined type. Meanwhile, BOAC was very keen to replace its outdated Avro Lancastrians and Yorks, which were basically conversions of Second World War Lancaster bombers. In order to compete with Pan Am, they purchased a number of American Boeing Stratocruisers for transatlantic services.

←A 1950 view of the Central Area with Terminal 1, the Queen's Building and control tower under construction. (Tom Singfield collection)

↓Lockheed L-1049E Super Constellation VT-DHL seen on one of its last visits to London Airport North in 1962. Air India inaugurated a weekly Bombay–London service via Cairo and Geneva on 8 June 1948, initially with the airline's L-749 Constellations, later replaced by these Super 'Connies'. From April 1960, Air India replaced its Super Constellations with Boeing 707s on the London route. VT-DHL went on to give faithful service with the Indian Air Force from June 1962 until November 1976, then with the Indian Navy until December 1983.

Plane spotters were encouraged to view the comings and goings at the new airport, as the government of the day wanted to promote air travel and air-mindedness, so a fenced enclosure was set up with tannoy broadcasts of the arrivals and departures being broadcast. All this occurred to the north of the main runway and became known as London Airport North.

Ian Allan was quick to spot a commercial opportunity and noticed that many trainspotters were now becoming interested in logging the airliners seen at London Airport. Having already produced books of locomotive numbers for trainspotters, it was now time to turn his attention to the fledgling 'plane spotters' and consequently the first issue of *Civil Aircraft Markings* appeared, with lists of all the airliners, airlines and civil aircraft to be seen in the UK, all ready to be marked off as 'seen'. With cameras and film still expensive for many, this was the ideal cheap way of recording what you saw.

Meanwhile, soon after the airport opened with its rudimentary facilities, work was progressing on the next phase and expansion of the airport to include a Central Area with new air traffic control tower, permanent terminal building complete with roof gardens and spectators' viewing terrace. Among the other facilities, new engineering maintenance bases were constructed for BEA and for BOAC.

The rest of the runways were completed, which formed a Star of David pattern, allowing take-offs and landings to be completed with any change of wind direction. A small permanent London North Terminal building was constructed in 1950, which replaced the tents. However, the parking space got pretty crowded at London Airport North in the early 1950s, so construction of the new terminal buildings in the Central Area got under way, together with a new air traffic control tower. British architect Frederick Gibberd was appointed to design permanent buildings for the airport. His plan saw the creation of a Central Area that was accessed via a vehicular tunnel running underneath the original main runway. The focal point of Gibberd's plan was a 122ft-high control tower. With the completion of the Central Area, operations were diverted from London Airport North, which became relegated to a cargo area and for small charter flights. On 17 April 1955, Her Majesty the Queen opened the new control tower at Terminal 1, which was named the Queen's Building, and Terminal 2, named the 'Europa Building' and serving the European airlines. She then returned to inaugurate the Central Terminal Area on 16 December.

A new BOAC headquarters building was planned and constructed in time for the Central Terminal Area's official opening in 1955. It consisted

↑The move to the Central Area takes place, with cranes finishing the final construction of the Queen's Building on the left in 1955.

↓Now in full operation, seen here is the Central Area, with two SAS DC-6Bs and a BEA Ambassador in the foreground of this 1955 aerial shot.

←A view of the Central Area looking east *c.* 1955, with seven BEA DC-3s visible in the foreground and the new BEA engineering base in the distance.

LONDON AIRPORT GUIDE

FOR VISITORS TO EUROPE'S LARGEST CIVIL AIRPORT

COMPLETE GUIDE FOR AIRCRAFT SPOTTERS

1'6

Airport Map + Aircraft Registration Numbers
How the Airport Works + About the Airlines
+ All Information Required by the Visitor

↑The 1955 London Airport official guidebook included a list of airline fleets and their aircraft for plane spotters to log.

←A panoramic view of the newly opened Central Area in 1955 looking west. (Tom Singfield collection)

⬆With the connecting tunnel nearing completion, the new Central Area control tower is seen on exit to the south in the early 1950s. (Tom Singfield collection)

⬇A view of the connecting traffic tunnel entrance looking north from the newly completed control tower in 1957. A Viscount can be seen getting airborne in the distance.

⬆A 1957 view of the new Central Area control tower with BEA RF4 buses parked in the foreground.

↑Part of the radar room inside the control tower in the 1960s showing the Precision Approach Radar controllers. (CAA Archives via Pete Bish)

→The visual control room in the air traffic control tower in the 1960s. (CAA Archives via Pete Bish)

←Boeing Stratocruiser G-AKGM *Castor* stands proudly outside the newly built BOAC headquarters hangar at Heathrow in 1955. (BOAC via Mike Stroud)

of two pairs of hangar pens, an engineering hall 800ft long and 90ft wide, with an attached eight-storey office block. At the time, the hangar was believed to be the largest in the world and could accommodate twelve Bristol Britannias at once as well as having a vast range of stores and working accommodation for about 4,000 personnel.

Meanwhile, BEA had started up over at nearby Northolt operating DC-3s and Vikings, and once the new London Airport was established, it

↑Boeing Stratocruiser G-AKGK of BOAC is seen on finals to Runway 28L wearing experimental BOAC titles in 1955.

←Inside the huge BOAC maintenance base is Stratocruiser G-AKGK *Canopus* receiving attention to its Pratt & Whitney R-4360 Double Wasp piston engines. (BOAC)

↓The BOAC engineering base with a Canadair Argonaut outside in 1959.

↑The 1956 official guidebook gave a hint of things to come, featuring an artist's impression of a turboprop BOAC Bristol Britannia on the cover.

↑A BOAC advertisement for the new Bristol Britannia, dubbed 'the whispering giant'.

moved in there, with an impressive engineering base, erected in 1952–53, awaiting them. This was claimed to be the largest prestressed concrete structure in Europe at the time, being about 1,000ft long with five hangar pens in each of two arms.

By now BEA was operating Vikings and DC-3s and by the mid 1950s, was starting to take delivery of its first Vickers Viscounts, which was a big step in air travel, being the first turboprop airliner to operate from London's Airport. However, the big piston-engined airliners lasted well into the 1960s with many airlines.

Following the opening of the Central Area, London Airport North's terminal building was demolished around 1965 and all use of that area ceased.

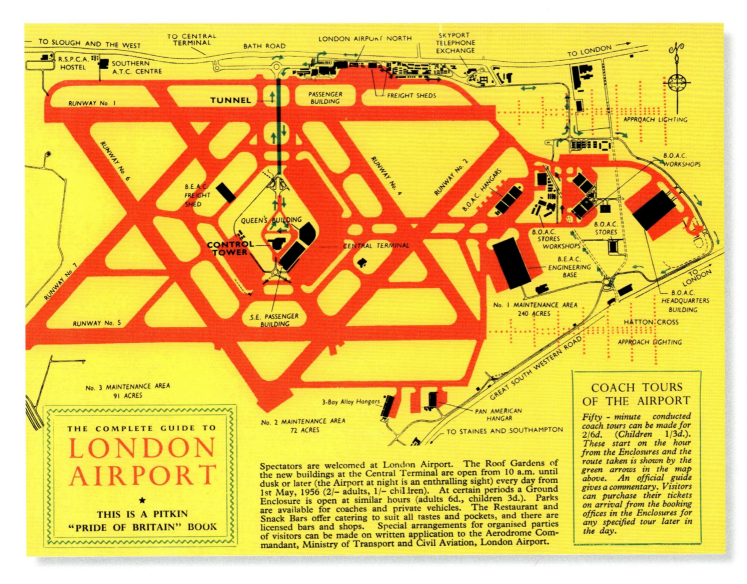

COACH TOURS OF THE AIRPORT

Fifty - minute conducted coach tours can be made for 2/6d. (Children 1/3d.). These start on the hour from the Enclosures and the route taken is shown by the green arrows in the map above. An official guide gives a commentary. Visitors can purchase their tickets on arrival from the booking offices in the Enclosures for any specified tour later in the day.

THE COMPLETE GUIDE TO
LONDON AIRPORT
★
THIS IS A PITKIN "PRIDE OF BRITAIN" BOOK

Spectators are welcomed at London Airport. The Roof Gardens of the new buildings at the Central Terminal are open from 10 a.m. until dusk or later (the Airport at night is an enthralling sight) every day from 1st May, 1956 (2/– adults, 1/– children). At certain periods a Ground Enclosure is open at similar hours (adults 6d., children 3d.). Parks are available for coaches and private vehicles. The Restaurant and Snack Bars offer catering to suit all tastes and pockets, and there are licensed bars and shops. Special arrangements for organised parties of visitors can be made on written application to the Aerodrome Commandant, Ministry of Transport and Civil Aviation, London Airport.

←The rear cover of the 1956 guidebook showed a plan of the airport at the time, with entrance prices to the spectators' viewing terraces and also for airport coach tours.

FOUR

GREAT VARIETY OF SIGHTS AND SOUNDS

As airliner technology progressed, more of the first-generation jets appeared – Boeing 707s, DC-8s, Comets and Caravelles intermingled with the shrill whistle of the Rolls-Royce Dart turboprop engines of the Vickers Viscounts, which were now becoming increasingly popular with many airlines. In 1959, the first airline to order the Fokker F27 Friendship was Aer Lingus. The type shared the same Rolls-Royce Dart engine as the Viscount, and for many years these were the only F27s seen at Heathrow.

After the much publicised Comet 1 crashes, trials were carried out by the Ministry of Supply with a pair of improved Comet 2s. Here is Comet 2E G-AMXD outside the original BOAC hangars in 1954. (Brian Stainer)

The much improved Comet 4 entered service with BOAC on the transatlantic route to New York in 1959. Here is G-APDM having one of its wingtip pinion fuel tanks inspected at the BOAC maintenance base. (BOAC)

↑An aerial view of the Europa Building, renamed Terminal 2, with BEA Viscount 701 and a DC-3 in the foreground in 1957.

↑A 1958 view of the entrance to the Europa Terminal with flags of airlines and countries flying from its roof. As its name implied, this terminal served European airlines only.

↑Terminal 2's departures hall shortly after its opening in 1957.

↑A colour view showing check-in desks inside Terminal 2 in 1957.

←How close can you get? As soon as the Central Area was open, spectators were afforded unprecedented views of the airliners. This 1958 view shows two BEA Viscounts, an Ambassador and a Swissair DC-6 on the apron.

↓Soviet-built airliners were indeed a rare sight, but Aeroflot started a weekly Thursday service from Moscow with its new Tupolev Tu-104s in the early 1960s. Even rarer were the Tu-104s of Czechoslovak State Airlines (CSA), which operated five of them. Here is Tu-104A OK-LDB at Heathrow on a glorious summer's day, 18 June 1962.

➜A caption is hardly necessary for this photograph as all that is needed is seen painted on the aircraft as it taxies past in October 1964! BKS Air Transport was the second customer for the Avro 748 and operated five of the type, including G-ASPL, which was leased from Avro from April 1964 until it was sold to Skyways Coach-Air in March 1967. (R.G. Griggs)

➜Another Eastern Bloc airline equipped with Soviet-built airliners was Malév, the Hungarian national airline, whose Ilyushin IL-18 HA-MOH is seen on finals to Runway 28R in March 1966. It was one of six operated by the airline. (Paul Burge/ARD collection)

↑A Commer lorry loads freight on to Aer Lingus Douglas C-47A EI-AFA, prior to its departure to Ireland in 1961.

By the late 1950s, it was not only BEA that was operating Viscounts into London Airport; Air France was soon followed by Aer Lingus, Lufthansa, KLM (Koninklijke Luchtvaart Maatschappij) and Austrian Airlines. Piston-engined airliners shared the apron with the newer types right up until the mid 1960s, with DC-3s operated by BEA, Cambrian Airways, Starways and British Westpoint Airlines, among others.

The 1950s also saw another turboprop airliner appear at London Airport but with a different sound, as the first Bristol Britannias were delivered to BOAC, powered by four Bristol Proteus engines that did not have the distinctive 'whistle' of the Viscounts Dart engines.

↑A wintry but sunny setting in January 1963 sees Avro York G-AGNV, of Skyways of London on the southern apron at Heathrow. The following year, this aircraft made its last flight to be preserved by the Skyfame Aircraft Museum at Staverton (Gloucestershire Airport) and is now with the RAF Museum at Cosford, painted in RAF colours as MW100.

←Liverpool-based Starways had a fleet of DC-3s, DC-4s and a pair of Viscounts that they operated into Heathrow in the early 1960s. Here we see DC-3 G-AMPY in April 1963 with an interesting advertising hoarding behind the two BEA Vanguards stating 'Fly BOAC to New York – £15 down and twenty-four monthly instalments of £7 4s 1d'. G-AMPY still flies today, wearing RAF Transport Command colours in the hands of Classic Air Force at Coventry.

↙KLM secured the first export order for the Series 800 Viscount, purchasing nine V.803s including PH-VID seen here disembarking its passengers at Heathrow on 20 August 1966. Viscount services began from Amsterdam to London on 6 October 1957 and continued until 1966, when they were replaced by DC-9s, the fleet being sold to Aer Lingus. (Ken Brookes)

↓In this view from the Europa Building's roof gardens on 3 June 1957, A SABENA DC-3 taxies past as visitors wave farewell to friends and relatives.

↖ in 1959 no covered walkways were attached when the aircraft parked, but glass walkways were provided from the buses or passengers could just walk out to the aircraft.

↑SAS Douglas DC-6B SE-BDS from Sweden is refuelled whilst crowds of spectators look on from the viewing terraces of the Queen's Building in 1958. The small white cabin in the centre of the roof terrace housed the commentator who gave spectators a running commentary on what was happening in front of them, interspersed with music, usually by Glen Miller!

←The 1957 guidebook published by Ian Allan featured BEA's new Vickers Viscount, that would bring a new sound to Heathrow – the whistling Rolls-Royce Dart turboprop engine that would be heard for the next forty years!

↑A quiet moment on the roof gardens in 1958, with a pair of BEA Viscounts and a DC-3 in view. The cabin seen on the right housed the apron controller at the time.

↑Heathrow was akin to a holiday destination for plane spotters on a good summer's day. Here in 1957, spotters are provided with parasols and chairs on the roof gardens of the Europa Building, where a SAS Convair 340 BEA DC-3s and a Viscount are seen. (Tom Singfield collection)

←Newly delivered BEA Vickers V.806 Viscount G-AOYR taxies into its parking bay in 1958.

↑Another late 1950s view from the roof gardens of Terminal 2, with a Lufthansa Convair 340 and several BEA Viscounts visible.

↑Air France was an early customer for the Vickers Viscount, ordering twelve Series 700s in November 1961. F-BGNN was only the fourteenth aircraft to be built, delivered in October 1953. It is seen here at Heathrow in 1957 with a BEA Viscount and Icelandair DC-4 in the background. F-BGNN served Air France until it was sold in April 1960. (R.G. Griggs/Author's collection)

↑Soviet-built aircraft were rare visitors during the 1950s, and none more so than this Aeroflot Ilyushin IL-14 SSSR-L1729, depicted in 1957 with a BEA Viscount and Ambassador in the background. (R.G. Griggs/Author's collection)

→Newly delivered Convair 440 EC-AMV of Spanish national airline Iberia awaits another load of holidaymakers before departing in 1957. The airline purchased a total of seventeen of the type in several batches for services throughout Europe from Madrid. This particular aircraft gave faithful service until October 1972, when it was transferred to the Spanish Air Force, and had several subsequent owners until it crashed on 21 August 1992 near La Paz in Bolivia. (R.G. Griggs/Author's collection)

↑The arrival of General Serov at London Airport on 2 April 1956 in Tupolev Tu-104 SSSR-L5400 of Aeroflot caused a major sensation and excitement among plane spotters. Alas, the presence of armed guards discouraged close scrutiny during the plane's visit. A few years later, Aeroflot established a weekly service with its Tu-104s, sharing services to Moscow with BEA.

↑Douglas DC-6B HB-IBE of Swissair on a scheduled flight from Zurich in 1957. This aircraft gave faithful service until it was sold to Sterling Airways of Denmark in June 1962. It was damaged beyond repair in a heavy landing at Torslanda (Gothenburg) on 23 December 1967. (R.G. Griggs/Author's collection)

↑A SABENA Convair 440 is viewed from the apron controller's cabin, in 1958, situated on the roof of the Europa Building.

↑A classic 1957 Heathrow scene with SAS Douglas DC-6B SE-BDR *Sture Viking* awaiting its next load of passengers bound for Stockholm. A Lufthansa Convair 440 is seen in the background in front of a BOAC advertising board. This DC-6B was sold to the French Air Force in October 1961, with whom it crashed on Réunion Island in the Pacific on 10 March 1968. (R.G. Griggs/Author's collection)

↑Here we see Convair 440 OH-LRC of Finnair being refuelled in 1957 on arrival from Helsinki. Finnair operated nine Convairliners to replace their DC-3s from 1956 to 1972 and they were in turn replaced by Caravelles into Heathrow in the early 1960s. (R.G.Griggs/Author's collection)

↑BEA operated a fleet of Airspeed Ambassadors during the 1950s under their Elizabethan class names. Here G-ALZT is seen in 1957 being prepared for departure, whilst Alitalia Convair 340 I-DOGU taxies behind and a BEA Viscount and DC-3 look on. This Ambassador served with BEA from January 1952 until May 1958, when it was sold to BKS Air Transport at Newcastle. It was withdrawn from use in October 1967 and scrapped the following year. (R.G. Griggs/Author's collection)

↑Lufthansa Convair 440 D-ACIG basks in the summer sun of 1957, whilst an Air France Viscount arrives in the background. This aircraft saw another ten years with Lufthansa until finally being sold to JAT Yugoslav Airlines in March 1969. It then became a corporate aircraft with an American operator, in whose hands it overran the runway at Key West, Florida, on 16 April 1979 and was withdrawn from use. (R.G. Griggs/ Author's collection)

↑Swissair operated fourteen Convair 440 Metropolitans, of which HB-IMB named *Fribourg* was the first, delivered in June 1956. It is seen here being refuelled and turned-round by classic period vehicles in 1958. This aircraft was sold to the German Air Force in October 1967. After having several subsequent owners, it crashed in Mexico on 21 May 1981. (R.G. Griggs/Author's collection)

←If you were a plane spotter at London Airport, you didn't have to stop to eat – you were afforded a fine view of the apron from the restaurant in the terminal building. This 1958 view shows Alitalia Douglas DC-6B I-DIMB right outside, but you had to ensure the window was closed when it started up or smoke from the engines might ruin your appetite!

↓With a trio of BEA Viscounts in the background, a Hunting-Clan crew bus awaits the arrival of Vickers Viking G-AJFS of Airwork on a Tradair flight on 12 April 1958. This aircraft later went on to serve with Channel Airways until being withdrawn in May 1964 and broken up. (Steve Bond)

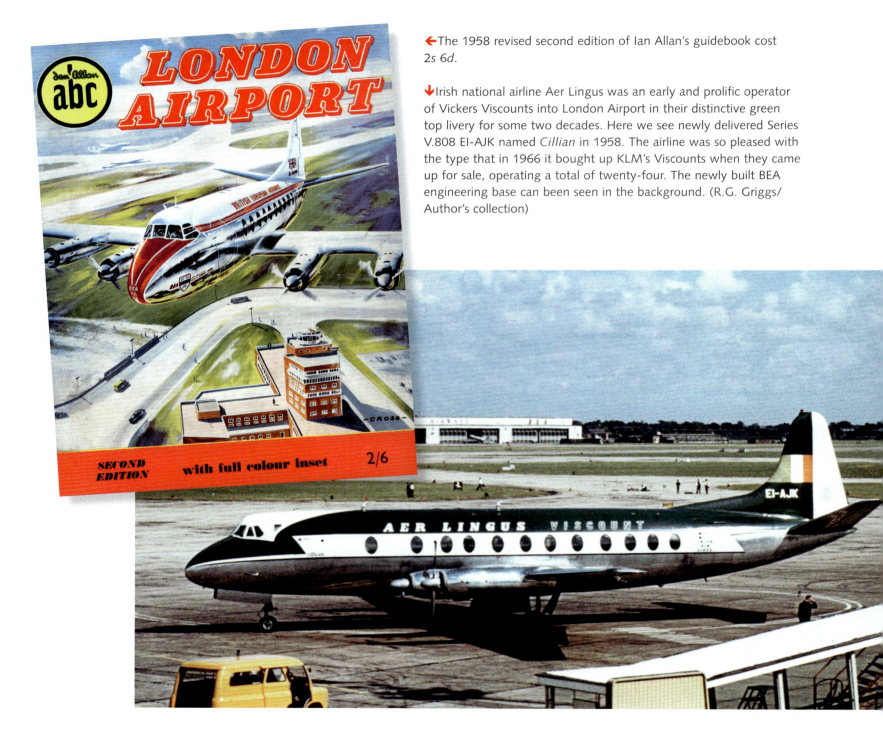

←The 1958 revised second edition of Ian Allan's guidebook cost 2s 6d.

↓Irish national airline Aer Lingus was an early and prolific operator of Vickers Viscounts into London Airport in their distinctive green top livery for some two decades. Here we see newly delivered Series V.808 EI-AJK named *Cillian* in 1958. The airline was so pleased with the type that in 1966 it bought up KLM's Viscounts when they came up for sale, operating a total of twenty-four. The newly built BEA engineering base can been seen in the background. (R.G. Griggs/Author's collection)

←The 1959 official guidebook featured one of BEA's Viscounts on the cover.

↓Douglas DC-3 G-AGZB was originally a Railway Air Services machine, joining BEA on 1 April 1947 when the airlines merged. Some seventy of the type were owned or leased for various periods until the last service by the type out of Heathrow on 19 May 1962. Named after British pioneers, G-AGZB *Pionair Robert Smith-Barry* is seen here at Heathrow in 1960, shortly before it crashed in a field near Elmdon, Birmingham, on 31 October. It was repaired and went on to see service with Channel Airways before crashing again on the Isle of Wight on 6 May 1962. In the distance can be seen Pan Am's cargo hangar with Yorks, a Viscount and a Viking just visible.

←A beautiful summer's day in 1957 as a BEA Elizabethen Class Airspeed Ambassador trundles past the newly delivered BEA Vickers V.701 Viscount G-AMON named *RMA Thomas Cavendish*. The Viscount was sold to Cambrian Airways in December 1962, then served with BOAC on its Scottish shuttle services, returning to BA when BEA and BOAC merged on 1 April 1974. Note the wide open spaces with only BEA's engineering base breaking the skyline at the time. (R.G. Griggs/ Stephen Wolf collection)

↓A BEA route map showing routes flown from Heathrow in the 1950s.

↑An early 1950s aerial view of the newly built BEA engineering base with Vickers Vikings lined up outside. (Tom Singfield)

↗A 1950s view inside BEA's engineering base with Viscounts and an Ambassador under maintenance. In 1953, BEA began receiving the first sixteen Viscount 701 turboprops it had ordered in August 1950. The first of these Discovery-Class aircraft entered service with forty-seven mixed-class seats in April 1953, and the first production aircraft (G-AMAV) went on to win the transport class of the 1953 London to Christchurch, New Zealand, air race, with BEA MD Peter Masefield as team manager and co-pilot.

→KLM was also an early Viscount customer and operator into Heathrow. here we see *Leonardo da Vinci*, V.803 Viscount PH-VIF, taxying out for Runway 28R in 1958 wearing the aircraft delivery scheme. (Paul Burge/ARD collection)

←A very rare colour photograph of BOAC Bristol Britannia 102, G-ANBA, on lease to Nigeria Airways, seen parked at London Airport North's apron in April 1959. (Paul Burge/ARD collection)

↓Awaiting its next load of passengers for holidaying in Greece in 1960 is Olympic Airways Douglas DC-6B SX-DAE. Olympic operated ten DC-6s until they were replaced on the London route by Comet 4Bs in the early 1960s. This particular DC-6 went on to serve Olympic on domestic routes until it crashed on Mount Pan, 46km north of Athens, on 8 December 1969. (Steve Bond)

Their sound was much quieter – so much so that the Britannia was called 'the whispering giant'. The Britannias started to replace the piston-engined Canadair Argonauts, DC-7Cs and Stratocruisers on BOAC's transatlantic routes and had completely replaced them by the end of the '50s.

On 4 October 1958, BOAC inaugurated the first jet-powered transatlantic service with their Comet 4, which commenced regular services later that year. The North Atlantic crossing still required a fuel stopover at Gander International Airport, Newfoundland. Despite the publicity it created by being first across the Atlantic on the London–New York route, Pan Am soon followed by the end of the year flying the Boeing 707. The DC-8 was also coming into service and both American jets would prove stiff competition for BOAC and the British airline industry as a whole, being larger, faster, longer-ranged and more cost-effective to operate than the Comet. In the end, BOAC succumbed and in 1958 purchased Boeing 707s – the successor to the Comet.

↑Fifteen years before BEA and BOAC merged to form BAs, BOAC Bristol Britannia 312 G-AOVG is seen here in front of the BOAC headquarters, having been leased to BEA in May 1961.

↗The 1960 official airport guidebook promoted the BOAC Comet 4's entry into service on the transatlantic route by including a build-and-fly cardboard model inside. The photograph of the BEA Viscounts on the cover was amended by an artist to show them in the new BEA colours.

➡Another Heathrow icon was the pride of BOAC – the Comet 4. Here we see G-APDT on its stand at Terminal 3 in 1965 shortly before its retirement, upon which it became a ground trainer, as depicted elsewhere in this book.

↑Rival to the Boeing 707 was Douglas's DC-8, similarly configured with four underslung Pratt & Whitney JT4A podded engines. Pan Am operated both Boeing 707s and DC-8s into Heathrow throughout the 1960s, with the last DC-8 service being in October 1968. Here is

DC-8-32 N811PA, named *Jet Clipper Pacific Trader*, in April 1967. Note the Perry Oaks Shell-BP bulk fuel storage tanks in the distance on the left. (Brian Stainer/APN)

↑The Boeing 707 made a big impact on the airline industry in the 1960s, and never more so than when BOAC ordered the type against the government's wishes for it to operate only British types. After some delays, BOAC was able to introduce its new 707s on to the London–New York route from 6 June 1960, followed by services to Montréal and Toronto on 18 August. The type was so well received that BOAC operated them into the early 1980s following the formation of BA. Here we see 707-436 G-APFD being refuelled prior to its next service in June 1962.

In June 1959, trials were conducted with the Fairey Rotodyne prototype, the world's first vertical take-off airliner. Powered by two Napier Eland turboprops for forward flight and a main rotor with tip-jets, it was hoped that BEA would operate the type between Heathrow and Battersea Heliport as well as to European cities. However, it was very noisy, and whilst Westland were busy consolidating other projects – having absorbed the Bristol Helicopter Division, Saunders Roe and Fairey Aviation in May 1960 – their marketing dithering caused potential customers to lose interest. A hoped-for military order was cancelled and in early 1962 funding was withdrawn for the project, resulting in the Rotodyne being broken up.

↓↘In June 1959, the sole Fairey Rotodyne prototype conducted trials between Battersea Heliport in Central London and Heathrow, in anticipation of BEA operating the type as the world's first vertical take-off airliner. However, due to the noise generated by the wing-tip jets and marketing failures, the project was abandoned, orders were cancelled and the aircraft was scrapped in January 1962.

←The first Vickers Vanguard to visit Heathrow was the first production aircraft, G-APEA, which conducted route-proving flights to Brussels and Rome in June 1959 wearing the livery of BEA, which was changed to the red square scheme in September of that year before delivery.

↓ On 1 March 1961, BEA began commercial services with the Vickers Vanguard, following a delay to the aircraft's entry into service as a result of major defects discovered in the Rolls-Royce Tyne engine's compressor during testing in early 1960. Following their delayed entry into service, BEA's Vanguards began flying to international destinations such as Malta and Barcelona and by 1962 had taken over approximately half of the flights previously operated by Viscounts on the airline's UK-domestic trunk routes, where they operated a 132-seat single-class configuration. The Vanguards' introduction on BEA's Heathrow–Scotland trunk routes increased traffic by more than 20 per cent. The first six Vanguards delivered had the small BEA red square logo applied to the tail, as seen on G-APEE shown here in January 1961, but soon this was enlarged across the rudder as shown elsewhere.

➜A pair of BEA AEC RF4 Regal buses and a Routemaster are depicted in 1962 awaiting their next load of passengers at Heathrow. BEA operated a unique variant of the Routemaster double-decker bus with forward passenger doors and towing a luggage trailer.

⬇It is clearly a very cold day in December 1961, as BEA Vanguard G-APEH is de-iced prior to departure. This aircraft now has the larger red square on its tail fin. Note the BOAC placard in the background advertising a £114 return fare to New York.

↑This is not just any old Vickers Viscount, this is G-APIM, which can be seen today preserved in the Brooklands Museum, Surrey. This view shows it in BEA's red square livery on 15 March 1962 with a BEA Argosy in the background. (Ken Brookes)

←↙The Comet 4B was tailored for BEA's requirements with lengthened fuselage for up to 100 passengers and shorter-span wings, devoid of the wingtip pinion fuel tanks, for higher speeds at mid-altitudes. BEA bought fourteen Comet 4Bs and introduced the type into service on 1 April 1960. In addition, Olympic Airways operated four aircraft in close co-operation with BEA, so that in effect their fleets were combined. Here we see G-ARJK being refuelled by an Esso Foden Pluto refueller on 15 March 1962. (Ken Brookes)

1959 saw a radical livery change for BEA, whose Viscounts, Vikings, Ambassadors and DC-3s were painted in a peony-red striped livery. Following the withdrawal of all its piston-engined fleet, BEA introduced the red square livery, which included painting the entire wings of its aircraft red. Its aircraft immediately became instantly recognisable both on the ground and in the air, and its new Vickers Vanguards, Comet 4Bs and Argosy freighters were delivered in the new scheme during the following years. Naturally, all ground support vehicles adopted the BEA red square livery in varying forms.

↑In 1961, BEA placed an order for three Armstrong Whitworth Argosy all-cargo aircraft. These were the airline's first dedicated freighters; the first aircraft was delivered and entered service later the same year. Four additional upgraded Series 222 Argosies were later purchased, including G-ATTC, seen here on 11 March 1967.

→A look inside the BEA engineering base hangar in 1965 reveals a Trident, Vanguard and three Comet 4Bs undergoing maintenance.

A new cargo terminal was constructed in the late 1950s, enabling dedicated cargo aircraft to be facilitated efficiently. Freighter Douglas DC-4s, DC-6s and Lockheed Constellations were frequent users in the 1950s, supplemented by such types as the Canadair CL-44s of Seaboard World Airlines and the Flying Tiger Line in the 1960s and former passenger-carrying Boeing 707s and Douglas DC-8s converted for cargo use.

➔The Shell Petroleum Aviation Division's fleet was based at Heathrow in the early 1960s. It comprised two Ambassadors, two Herons and a Dove. Their base was in the former Hunting-Clan hangars adjoining the Cargo Dock hangar. (Via Tom Singfield)

⬇The Seaboard World Cargo Dock hosted many cargo and freight carriers including Lebanese operator, Trans Mediterranean Airways Douglas DC-6B OD-AEY seen here in April 1966. (Brian Stainer/APN)

FIVE

THE 1960S – TRIUMPH AND TRAGEDY!

Over at Blackbushe Airport, Eagle Airways had been flourishing and expanding, acquiring a couple of Douglas DC-6s in 1959, to join its Vickers Viking fleet. In May 1960, Blackbushe closed to commercial traffic and Eagle moved its main operating and maintenance base to Heathrow, occupying the former BOAC hangars, which were parallel to Runways 5 and 23. Eagle had been operating regularly from Heathrow since 1957 and by the time of the move, most operations were already being conducted from there. Prior to the move, it was announced on 21 March 1960 that the Cunard

↑In March 1960, the Cunard Steamship Company bought a 60 per cent shareholding in Eagle Airways for £30 million, resulting in a change of name to Cunard Eagle Airways. Here we see Vickers V.707 Viscount G-ARKH wearing its new titles in June 1961. (Brian Stainer)

←Eagle Airways Vickers Viking G-AHPM in 1960, shortly after Eagle moved its operating base from Blackbushe to Heathrow. After the airline was renamed Cunard Eagle Airways, this aircraft crashed into Holteheia, near Stavanger, Norway, inbound from Heathrow on 9 August 1961. All thirty-nine occupants were killed.

←Another sad occasion when British Eagle International Airlines ceased operations, with the entire fleet parked up outside the company's hangar in November 1968. (BAA via Pete Bish)

→This superb shot shows Heathrow-based British Eagle at its best with Bristol Britannia 312 G-AOVN on finals to Runway 28R, whilst two more company Britannias can be seen sitting outside the Eagle hangars, on 31 July 1965. (Steve Bond)

Steamship Company had acquired a controlling interest in the Eagle Group of companies, but this takeover was not completed until 19 May 1960, by which time Cunard had purchased the entire share of the Eagle Group.

Meanwhile, in April, Eagle had acquired its first Bristol Britannia, leased from Cuban airline Cubana, followed by its first Viscount. The airline's name officially changed to Cunard Eagle Airways Ltd on 28 July 1960 and all aircraft subsequently adopted the new titles, as more Britannias and Viscounts joined the DC-6s, followed by a pair of Boeing 707s. This lasted until 1963, when Cunard concentrated its efforts and resources on an alliance with BOAC, resulting in Harold Bamberg, Eagle's owner, buying back 60 per cent of Cunard's shares on 16 September 1963. The airline was renamed British Eagle International Airlines Ltd in November 1961.

The whole of the north side terminal closed to passenger traffic around 1963. KLM was one of the last to leave even though it was a European short-haul operator. BOAC, Pan Am and TWA were phased out to the Central Oceanic Building during 1962.

Designed to handle long-haul routes for foreign carriers to the US, Asia and other Far Eastern destinations, the Central Oceanic Building was renamed Terminal 3 in 1968 and expanded in 1970 to add an arrivals building. Other facilities added included the UK's first moving walkways.

Terminal 1 opened in 1969, completing the cluster of buildings at the centre of the airport site, by which time 14 million passengers a year were passing through the airport. The jet age was in full swing, with Boeing 707s, DC-8s VC10s and Tridents taking travellers from Heathrow to and from all parts of the world.

←Terminal 3 was opened as the Oceanic Terminal on 13 November 1961. It was built to handle flight departures for long-haul routes. Renamed Terminal 3 in 1968, it was expanded in 1970 with the addition of an arrivals building.

↓G-ARPG heads a trio of BEA Trident 1Cs being refuelled in 1966 prior to their next service.

↙Inside Terminal 3 in 1969, we see the check-in desks for BOAC and QANTAS airlines.

←In 1968, BEA had a livery change from the red square scheme to this scheme called 'Speedjack'. Repainting all aircraft and equipment during a livery change is both timely and costly, but by February 1970 most of the fleet had been repainted as shown on Trident 1C G-ARPK at the start of its push-back from the line on departure.

↙This view from the side of the Queen's Building in 1971 shows a sea of BEA ground support vehicles resplendent in the salmon-red 'Speedjack' vehicle livery.

↓When airlines change the livery on their aircraft they tend to change everything else, including all the ground support equipment, such as these Bedford articulated buses. Photographed in April 1970, one is seen in BEA's old livery sandwiched between two in the new 'salmon-red' scheme.

The Airport Authority Act was passed in 1965, creating the British Airports Authority (BAA), which was to take responsibility for three state-owned airports: London Heathrow Airport, London Gatwick Airport and London Stansted Airport.

Another branding change came for BEA in 1968, when it disposed of the red square livery and replaced it with a new design called the 'Speedjack', basically a stylised Union Flag on a dark blue tail with a new BEA logo, but retaining the all-important red wings on its aircraft. This livery subsequently progressed to all BEA aircraft and vehicles, the latter of which were repainted in a garish salmon-red colour.

It was soon clear that with ever increasing freight and cargo flights the present cargo hangars were inadequate, so a new 160-acre (0.65km²) cargo terminal was constructed to the south of the southern runway in the late 1960s, managed by BEA, which connected to Terminals 1, 2 and 3 by a tunnel.

Although the 1960s were a boom time for the airport and airlines at Heathrow, there was one sad significant loss to the airport when British Eagle International Airlines ceased trading on 11 July 1968 and all flights by the airline ceased; the last flight was by Britannia G-AOVG from

↑BEA's fleet of AEC RF4 Regal one-and-a-half-deck buses were all retired by the time the airline changed its livery in 1968 to the 'Speedjack' scheme … all but one, MLL 740, which was repainted in the new BEA salmon-red colour making it very unique on the Heathrow Airport scene in August 1968. This bus has since been preserved by the Brooklands Bus Museum.

→By 1969, BEA carried 132,000 tonnes of freight each year. That year, it also opened a new cargo centre at Heathrow, which it jointly operated with BOAC. It can be seen behind this view of Transportes Aéreos Portugueses (TAP) Boeing 707-382B, CS-TBA on 19 December 1970. (Roger Braithwaite)

→↘An accident befell BOAC Boeing 707-465 G-ARWE en route from London Heathrow Airport to Sydney via Zurich and Singapore. On Monday 8 April 1968, it suffered an engine failure on take-off that quickly led to a major fire. The engine fell off the aircraft in flight. After the aircraft had made a successful emergency landing, confusion over checklists and distractions from the presence of a check captain contributed to the deaths of five of the 127 on board. (Brian Stainer/APN)

↑The carnage caused by BKS Ambassador, G-AMAD, crashing on to parked BEA Tridents at Heathrow on 3 July 1968. (BAA via Pete Bish)

Amsterdam on 7 November 1968. The hangars and offices were closed for the last time on Friday 8 November. Started as Eagle Airways, the airline had been part of the Heathrow scene for some ten years and Eagle's black hangars were a prominent feature on the scene.

Financial loss and the collapse of an airline is one thing but physical loss of an airliner and more importantly life is quite another. Today, the advances in aircraft design, technology, equipment and training mean that airline travel is safer than ever, but Heathrow has suffered its share of tragedies over the years.

On Monday 8 April 1968, BOAC Flight 712 (callsign Speedbird 712) was a BOAC service operated by Boeing 707-465 G-ARWE from London Heathrow Airport bound for Sydney via Zurich and Singapore. On take-off it suffered an engine failure that quickly led to a major fire, following which the engine fell off the aircraft in flight. After the aircraft had made a successful emergency landing, fire spread throughout the aircraft. Although the majority of passengers were safely evacuated, confusion over checklists and distractions from the presence of a check captain contributed to the deaths of five of the 127 on board.

The actions taken by those involved in the accident resulted in the award of the George Cross posthumously to stewardess Barbara Jane Harrison. Two other crew members received awards: a BEM and an MBE. As a direct result of the accident, BOAC changed the checklists for severe engine failures and engine fires, combining them both into one checklist, the Engine Fire or Severe Failure Checklist.

Three months later, on 3 July 1968, Airspeed Ambassador, registration G-AMAD, of BKS Air Transport, crashed at London Heathrow Airport, damaging two parked Trident airliners as it cartwheeled into the incomplete London Heathrow Terminal 1, then under construction. Six of the eight people on board the Ambassador were killed, along with the eight racehorses being transported.

The Ambassador had recently been converted to a horsebox transport and was on a flight from Deauville, France to Heathrow Airport. It was transporting eight racehorses belonging to businessman William Hill and five grooms. As the aircraft was landing on Heathrow's Runway 28R, the left wing dropped, and the wing tip and left landing gear touched the grass adjacent to the runway. The crew tried to increase power to go-around and climb away, but the bank angle increased. The aircraft hit two parked empty BEA Hawker Siddeley Tridents, knocking the tail fin off one (G-ARPI) and slicing off the entire tail section of the other (G-ARPT). The Ambassador cartwheeled following the impact and slid upside down, coming up against the ground floor of the terminal building, resulting in an explosion.

Six people on board the Ambassador died, including the flight crew and three of five grooms, along with all eight horses. The other two grooms were seriously injured as were two people on the ground. A further twenty-nine people on the ground sustained slight injuries. Of the two Trident aircraft, G-ARPT was damaged beyond economic repair and G-ARPI was subsequently repaired but was later destroyed when it crashed on 18 June 1972 in what became known as the Staines Air Disaster.

SIX

PLANE SPOTTER'S PARADISE

The author's first visit to London Heathrow was with his parents and grandfather in 1959, followed by a school visit the following year. By then the 'bug' had bitten and a return visit in 1961 became serious stuff, with a copy of Ian Allan's *Civil Aircraft Markings*, a pen and binoculars all being mandatory equipment for this fledgling plane spotter!

↑The author offers no apologies for including this photograph depicting Ilyushin IL-14 SP-LNG of LOT Polish Airlines arriving at its parking bay on 7 August 1961. This was the first Soviet-built aircraft the author had seen and he still recalls his father's excited exclamation when he saw it: 'Christ, it's a "Crate"!' 'Crate' was the NATO reporting name for the IL-14. (Eric A.J. Balch)

←The author, aged 11, poses proudly on the spectators' terrace in front of Loftleidir Douglas DC-6B TF-LLA on 7 August 1961. A blazer, clean shirt and tie were the order of the day for this important occasion!

⬇Wrap up warm, take your spotting logbooks, pen and binoculars and get your mum to pack your sandwiches. Then you were all set for a day's plane spotting with your mates on Heathrow's viewing terraces in the 1960s. A far healthier activity than sitting at home playing computer games and one many still enjoy, whatever their age.

Ian Allan
a b c

LONDON AIRPORT
2/6

⬆The 1961 official guidebook also featured BEA's Vickers Vanguard on the cover, as it took delivery of the first of twenty of the type.

↑KLM leased Lockheed Electra PH-LLD to Air Ceylon
(now Air Lanka) for one year from 1 November 1960 to
1 November 1961. It is seen here during a rare visit in April
1961, viewed from the Queen's Building.

→The first Airbus? An Air France publicity photo was staged
at Heathrow in April 1965 featuring two double-deckers-
Breguet 763 Deux Ponts, F-BASQ and a London Transport RT
double-decker bus. (Brian M. Service via Pete Bish)

A very rare surprise for plane spotters occurred on 25 April 1956, when three Russian Aeroflot Tu-104s arrived on a route-proving flight to London Airport. (Brian M. Service via Pete Bish)

↑What logbooks were they filling in? Why, the annual Ian Allan *Civil Aircraft Markings* books that listed all the airliners likely to be seen at Heathrow. Here are the author's copies throughout the 1960s.

←The view on a murky wet day in April 1966 with the old Heathrow control tower in the background. Who would have thought that fifty years ago, Syrians came to the UK in this classic pristine vintage Douglas C-54A Skymaster? However, with the double doors open on the rear fuselage it is thought this was on a freight flight rather than transporting tourists or even refugees! YK-ADA was the sole remaining C-54 operated by Syrian Arab Airlines and was written off at Damascus six months later. (Brian Stainer/APN)

↙BEA operated a unique fleet of AEC RF4 Regal one-and-a-half-deck coaches to take passengers from the centre of London to the airport. SOme of them are seen here lined up in from the Europa Terminal in the early 1960s.

↓More BEA buses and a full car park viewed from the Queen's Building in 1961 in the days before the multi-storey car parks.

By then, the old terminal on the north side had been relegated to charter and cargo operator, whilst the main scheduled airlines now operated from either the Europa Terminal (later renamed Terminal 2) or the Oceanic Terminal (now Terminal 3). In 1955 Her Majesty the Queen opened the office block, which was appropriately named the Queen's Building. All these buildings were equipped with roof terraces and gardens, a café and shops, all promoting airline travel and aviation. There was even a children's paddling pool on the roof and a playground with amusements to keep the younger members of the family entertained whilst Dad did the serious stuff watching the planes!

This was paradise for the aviation enthusiasts of the day, as the aircraft parked right alongside and you were looking right down on them, watching passengers embarking and disembarking.

↓A 1961 aerial view of the Central Area, with Lufthansa Viscount D-ANUN, in the foreground. (Tom Singfield collection)

← 22 June 1963: the Europa Building was also called the No.1 Passenger Building. (Lee Holden)

↙ Two years later, to avoid confusion the name on the wall was changed to 'No.1 Building Europa'. On the viewing terrace roof, flags of the many airlines it served were flown. (Lee Holden)

↓ Inside the Europa Terminal: ticket and check-in desks are seen in this view on 5 February 1960.

➜Another terminal building interior view on the same day shows the Forte café, Barclays bank and other facilities.

⬇Canadair C-4 Argonaut VR-AAT was one of three bought from BOAC by Aden Airways and is seen at London Airport North in June 1960. It was previously registered G-ALHV and operated with the airline for three years, clearly retaining the basic BOAC colours. (Paul Burge/ARD collection)

⬂Passengers board Aer Lingus V.808 Viscount EI-AJI in July 1963, whilst Kuwait airline Trans Arabia Airways' DC-6B gets towed past. (Steve Bond)

↖Seen taxying out in October 1963 past an Aer Lingus Viscount and SAS Caravelle is newly delivered BOAC Vickers VC10 G-ARVF, which was the sixth production aircraft of the thirteen ordered by the airline. (R.G. Griggs)

↑A very busy car park with period taxies in the foreground, viewed from the Queen's Building in July 1963. (Courtesy Lee Holden)

←For many years, KLM was the only operator of the Lockheed Electra into London Airport; it had eleven of them. PH-LLB, named *Venus*, is seen here in April 1963.

↑A misty morning in 1964 and Lufthansa V.814D Viscount D-ANAF departs with the Queen's Building and control tower both in view. Lufthansa had eleven Viscounts which were daily visitors to Heathrow throughout the 1960s. This particular aircraft was withdrawn from use on 30 January 1969 and has been used for ground apprentice training at Frankfurt ever since. (Courtesy Lufthansa)

⬆ When BEA sold some of its early 700 Series Viscounts to Cambrian Airways, Cambrian conveniently retained BEA's red wing colours. Cambrian purchased G-AMNZ from BEA in June 1963, and on 20 January 1964 inaugurated a Liverpool–Heathrow service. G-AMNZ was finally withdrawn and broken-up at Cardiff in September–October 1971.

↑By August 1964, when this photograph was taken, BEA had received its full fleet complement of twenty Rolls-Royce Tyne turboprop-powered Vanguards including G-APEL. It continued in service after the formation of British Airways on 1 April 1974, being sold to French operator Europe Aero Service two years later and finally to Air Gabon in January 1980 as a cargo aircraft.

↑Soviet-built airliners were operated by all the airlines of Eastern Bloc countries into Heathrow during the 1960s. LOT Polish Airlines flew Ilyushin IL-18s, which were the most common. It operated nine of the type for over thirty years, including SP-LSB, seen here arriving from Warsaw in May 1964. (R.G. Griggs)

↑The 1964 official guidebook, featuring a BEA Comet 4B on the cover.

➔A passenger's-eye view of the Queen's Building and BEA Viscount G-AOYO. taken from BEA Vanguard G-APEM, in May 1964.

↖The German national airline Lufthansa was the first operator of the Boeing 727 in Europe, commencing services to London on 16 April 1964 with one aircraft operating a Hamburg–London–Dusseldorf service. On 10 May 1964, a Frankfurt–London route was established. Lufthansa operated sixteen Boeing 727-30s, followed by another ten 727-30QC variants (quick change) that had a freight door for cargo. D-ABIG, one of the early ones, is seen taxying in November 1965.

↑Probably the last visit to Heathrow by Swissair Douglas DC-3, HB-IRX in 1962, shortly before its retirement. Swissair ordered its Original five DC-3s before the Second World War and introduced a non-stop Zurich–London route, one of the longest routes at the time. After the Second World War, many former military DC-3s and C-47s became available, and the DC-3 quickly became the most important airplane in the post-war fleets of most airlines, including Swissair. (Courtesy Paul Burge/ARD)

←Happy times on a summer's day in July 1967 as children are occupied by the viewing terrace amusements, whilst no doubt the control tower staff's attention is concentrated on the BOAC Boeing 707 getting airborne in the distance. From the 1950s to the 1970s, everything was done to ensure all the family was catered for, and aviation and airline travel was promoted, unlike today, when spectators at Heathrow are not made welcome!

↑Esso sponsored these three foldout London Airport guide maps issued in 1962, '65 and '68. A plan of the airport was on one side and on the other were coloured profile drawings of most of the airliners and airlines seen at the airport at the time.

On reaching the spectators' viewing terraces, it was fascinating to watch the larger four piston-engined airliners start up, such as the DC-6s and DC-7Cs of Swissair, SAS and Alitalia, as well as the Super Constellations of Air France, QANTAS, Trans-Canada Airlines, TWA and others.

Clouds of blue smoke would be emitted from each Pratt & Whitney or Wright Turbo Compound piston engine, as the props turned, one by one and the giant airliner spluttered into life like a fire-breathing dragon. A similar sight would attract attention to the Convair 340 and 440 twin-engined piston airliners that operated frequent schedules by Swissair, Lufthansa, Finnair, Société Anonyme Belge d'Exploitation de la

↑Piston-engined airliners became an increasingly rare sight at London Heathrow towards the end of the 1960s, as they were retired and replaced by more modern turbo-prop and jet types. This Douglas DC-6B TF-FIP, named *Solfaxi*, was still in service with Icelandair when photographed in November 1966. A Cambrian Airways Viscount sits opposite and in the distance can be seen the British Eagle fleet of Britannias and a Viscount outside their base. (R.G. Griggs)

←Lockheed L-749A Constellation G-ANUR was originally delivered to QANTAS in 1947, before being sold to BOAC in 1955. It was initially leased to Skyways of London in 1959, but the company bought it outright in 1962. It is seen here taxying out in June 1962, wearing the airline's smart duck-egg green and red trim. In the background can be seen the Eagle hangars with the fleet of Cunard Eagle Airways Britannias amongst others. (Tom Singfield collection)

←Air France had a large fleet of different variants of the Lockheed Constellation and became the last operator of the type into London Heathrow, the last being in July 1967. F-BHML was a L-1049G Super Constellation, seen here in April 1965 on a freight flight. The final five Super Constellations were retired by Air France on 2 October 1967. (John Roger collection)

→BOAC variety in 1965: a Comet 4, Boeing 707-436 G-ARRC operated by BOAC-Cunard and VC10 G-ARVA leased to Nigeria Airways all lined up at Terminal 3. Beyond these can be discerned a Comet 4C of Middle East Airlines and a pair of Pan Am DC-8s.

Navigation Aérienne (SABENA) and Iberia. It is interesting to note that all these major flag-carrying airlines are not only still operating, but still fly into Heathrow today, apart from SABENA, which ceased operations in 2001. (Trans-Canada Airlines changed its name to Air Canada in 1965.)

The first jets seen at London Airport were the Comet 1s of BOAC in the early 1950s, followed by the Boeing 707s of Pan Am and Comet 4s of BOAC at the end of the 1950s, competing on the transatlantic route. The first successful short-haul jet was the French Caravelle, which had great passenger appeal, due to its rear-mounted Rolls-Royce Avon engines, rear-mounted folding stairs and unique triangular-shaped passenger windows. It also shared the same nose as the British de Havilland Comet. Air France, Swissair, SAS, Alitalia, Iberia, TAP, Austrian Airlines and Finnair were the first European airlines to operate the type into London Airport from the early 1960s and if you didn't see at least one from each airline during your visit, you were having a bad day!

Of course the viewing terraces were not just for plane spotters; it was a good day out for the family, just watching the comings and goings of international airliners. On the roof of the Queen's Building was a small

↑Seen outside the BOAC headquarters in May 1966 is Comet 4 G-APDM, when ended up as a ground handling training airframe with Dan-Air at Gatwick Airport. (R.G. Griggs)

↑A classic icon in its element: Pan Am Boeing 707-321B N423PA *Clipper Glory of the Skies* is seen on finals to Runway 28R on 24 January 1971. Pan Am introduced this variant on the New York–Heathrow route for the first time on 10 October 1959, which enabled it to fly direct without the refuelling stop at Gander that had previously been necessary with the 707-120 variant. Pan Am's 707s were seen daily at Heathrow until the mid 1970s when they were replaced by Boeing 747s.

⬆French-built Sud Aviation Caravelles were a familiar sight at Heathrow during the 1960s and '70s from European operators, including Alitalia, whose Caravelle VIN I-DABR *Bellatrix* is seen taxying out in May 1964. Alitalia had twenty-one Caravelles that operated routes throughout Europe. This particular aircraft was withdrawn from use and broken up in October 1965. Note the Ghana Airways Bristol Britannia in the top-left outside the Eagle hangars. (R.G. Griggs)

⬆Another name that has been a feature of the Heathrow scene for some sixty years is Scandinavian Airlines System, whose fleet has always been split between Denmark, Norway and Sweden, with aircraft registered accordingly. Here we see Norwegian-registered Caravelle III LN-KLH, named *Trygve Viking*, basking in the autumn sun in September 1966.

⬆Another Swissair airliner, this time Sud Aviation SE 210 Caravelle III HB-ICZ, one of seven operated by the airline, taxies out in June 1962. The BEA Commer truck alongside the BEA Vickers Vanguard in the foreground had one of the least glamorous jobs on the airport – emptying the aircraft toilets after each arrival!

glass cabin in which an announcer was situated, broadcasting information about the arrivals and departures as they occurred. This was interspersed with music tannoyed over the terraces, making the whole experience enjoyable. The author recalls one such occasion he happened to be there when a Swissair DC-8 made its first appearance at the airport. The announcer had never seen one before and described it as a 'Boeing 707', to which a knock on the door and polite correction by the author put the announcer right and the announcement was corrected!

The author also recalls a rather wet day in the mid 1960s when, at the tender age of 16, he was climbing the stairs inside the Queen's Building to the viewing terraces on a plane spotting trip, armed with notebooks, binoculars and sandwiches. Almost at the top of the stairs, he was met by a horde of hysterical screaming girls, some of whom were crying, 'Don't

↑Austrian Airlines had five Caravelle VI-Rs in its fleet, including OE-LCE *Tyrol*, seen here in May 1964 keeping company with newly delivered BEA Trident 1C G-ARPK. (Stephen Wolf)

→In 1967, SAS modified its livery, reducing the 'Scandinavian Airlines System' roof titles to just 'Scandinavian' and changing the trim to a lighter blue, as seen on Danish-registered Caravelle III OY-KRF *Torkil Viking*, overlooked by plenty of spectators on the balconies of the Queen's Building behind on a bright morning in April 1967. Note the white announcer's cabin on the balcony, from where all arrivals and departures were broadcast. (Brian Stainer/APN)

leave me John.' I thought, 'my name's not John', until I was told that the Beatles were leaving for America. I wasn't bothered about the Beatles, as getting my first photograph of a brand new TAP Boeing 707 was far more important!

→Another significant picture depicts the last former BOAC Canadair Argonaut G-ALHJ, seen here sitting outside the BEA Engineering Base on 31 July 1965 awaiting its fate as a fire service training airframe. It lasted intact until 1979, when it was finally destroyed in an exercise. (Steve Bond)

←With the Ground Support Equipment vehicles all wearing the new BEA livery, Viscount G-AOYS is still awaiting a repaint into the BEA 'Speedjack' scheme in 1969, as spectators look on from the Queen's Building.

BOAC
AND BOAC CUNARD
route map and flight information

Services operated for BOAC-CUNARD by BOAC

↖In 1965, BOAC changed its livery to that shown here on VC10 G-ARVK, outside the BOAC hangar in April that year. Nicknamed the 'Meat Cleaver' scheme, the 'stepped' cheatline was short-lived and was soon modified to a sweeping smooth curve. (R.G. Griggs)

↑1960s BOAC VC10 in-flight brochure.

←A selection of London Airport's official guidebooks from the 1950s and '60s.

←Very rare visitors to Heathrow were the Soviet Tupolev Tu-114s of Aeroflot, which only made one or two visits, this one being SSSR-76485 in July 1966. It is surrounded by an unusually large number of curious BEA ground support vehicles! (Brian Stainer via Tom Singfield)

↙April 1967: a pair of Bedford KLM passengers buses is parked alongside Lufthansa Boeing 727-30, D-ABIL, whilst a Douglas DC-6B of Loftleidir Icelandic Airlines passes behind.

↓This South African Airways Boeing 707-344 is seen parked up at Terminal 3 in 1966, being serviced by period BOAC ground service equipment vehicles including a Commer hydraulic elevated catering truck on the left. Directly behind the 707 is a Comet 4C of Kuwait Airways. (Via Tom Singfield)

↖A cold day in January 1967 sees this Japan Air Lines Douglas DC-8-32 JA8005 named *Miyajima* inbound from Tokyo. (Brian Stainer/APN)

↑In 1963, ten redundant RF buses were sold to BEA, which fitted them with communications equipment and flashing roof lights for working airside at Heathrow. Here one is seen scurrying out of the tunnel inbound to the terminal building with another load of passengers from London.

←Along with Pan Am, TWA also became an iconic sight at Heathrow, initially with Lockheed Constellations during the 1950s and then with a huge fleet of Boeing 707s. Here we see 707-331B N774TW moments before touchdown on Runway 28R on 29 July 1967. (Steve Bond)

←Middle East Airlines of Lebanon leased this VC10 9G-ABP from Ghana Airways on 1 April 1967, but it was destroyed in an Israeli raid on Beirut on 28 December 1968. It is seen here departing from Terminal 3 in May 1968. (R.G. Griggs)

➔After operating Super Constellations into London throughout the 1950s, Air India replaced them with Boeing 707s and 707-337B VT-DSI is seen on finals to Runway 28R on 11 August 1968. Note the last former Canadair Argonaut G-ALHJ in the distance; it was used as a fire crew ground trainer. (Stephen Wolf)

↖In 1968, Lufthansa repainted the tail fins on its aircraft dark blue with a large logo, which it retains today. Here we see two Boeing 727-30s in July 1968, D-ABIJ with the new blue tail colour, and D-ABIU behind with the old tail scheme.

↑Another view that shows just how close the spectators' viewing terrace was to the action on Terminal 2, as two husbands share the delights of 'plane spotting' with their wives in 1969. A telephoto lens was not required in order to take good photographs as this shot of TAP Boeing 727-82 CS-TBM shows. (Ken Guest)

←The most successful Boeing airliner to date has been the 737, which has been seen in greater numbers at Heathrow than any other type. Here we see Boeing 737-130 D-ABEY *City Jet Warms* of Lufthansa, sharing the apron with a Convair 990 Coronado of Swissair and two more Lufthansa planes – a Boeing 727 and another 737 – in June 1969.

➜Another photograph emphasising the wonderful viewing facilities in the 1960s; they lasted until the late 1990s. Here we see KLM's Douglas DC-9-32 PH-DNK in 1969. (Ken Guest)

➜Heads of state were frequent visitors to Heathrow when visiting London. Here we see *Air Force One*, the US president's Boeing VC-137C 62-6000, on 22 January 1969, when it brought in newly elected President Richard Nixon to meet Her Majesty the Queen and Prime Minister Harold Wilson. (Richard Andrews collection)

SEVEN

THE 1970S – A NEW ERA

The world became even smaller in the 1970s thanks to Concorde and wide-body jets such as the Boeing 747, the first of which landed at Heathrow on 12 January 1970 to commence service for Pan Am. By the end of the decade, 27 million passengers were using Heathrow annually.

The day of the 1 July 1972 was an exciting date for Heathrow, being the day Concorde made its second visit, when 002 G-BSST arrived during its test programme. This gave BOAC staff an opportunity to see what they

←By 1971, some of BEA's Vanguards had been converted to all-cargo freighters and redesignated Merchantmen, such as G-APEL, seen here on finals on 24 January 1971.

↑An aerial view in 1970 looking north-east. Terminal 3 is seen in the foreground with a QANTAS Boeing 707.

expected to be operating in a few years time. However, two years later, 1974 saw a big shake-up in the British airline industry, as BEA and BOAC merged to form British Airways (BA) on 1 April 1974, incorporating the airlines within the British Air Services Group, Newcastle-based Northeast Airlines (formerly BKS Air Transport) and Cardiff-based Cambrian Airways. It would be more than a year to change the liveries and logos on all aircraft, vehicles and buildings to the new Negus-designed BA livery, and many flew in hybrid schemes until it was their turn for a repaint. The old BEA and BOAC founding names at Heathrow were now history.

Carried on the
First Flight from London Airport
THE PAN AM BOEING 747
"Young America"
Nº1 London Proving Flight
12th Jan 1970

Arlington Supplies
291 Green Lanes
Palmers Green
London, N.13 England

↑A major milestone in Heathrow's history came in January 1970 with the arrival of the first Boeing 747 jumbo jet. Operated by Pan Am, a proving flight was carried out on 12 January 1970.

←An aerial view of how Heathrow Airport looked in 1972. (BAA)

↑Following the first Boeing 747 route-proving flight, this was followed on 22 January 1970 by the first passenger-carrying 747 service, when N736PA *Clipper Victor* touched down at 1414GMT – seven hours late due to technical problems resulting in an aircraft change. The jumbo had brought in 324 passengers across the Atlantic from New York to London. Here is Pan Am's 747-121, N737PA *Clipper Young America* – the aircraft originally planned for the inaugural flight – on finals to Runway 09 on 31 March 1974, four years later.

By 1971, there were still some BEA aircraft that had not been repainted in the new 'Speedjack' livery, which had been adopted in 1968. These were mainly some of the Vickers Vanguards that were soon due for retirement, including G-APEA, shown here on finals to Runway 28L on 4 February 1971. Indeed G-APEA was withdrawn from use on 19 December 1972 and broken up the following year. G-APEA was the flagship of BEA and was the first production Vanguard, shown earlier in this book during route-proving trials in June 1959.

Vickers Super VC10 G-ASGO of BOAC is seen here being turned round at Terminal 3 in 1971.

When BEA and BOAC merged to form BA on 1 April 1974, both fleets had to be repainted in the new livery, but so did all the ground support equipment including BEA's luggage-trailer-towing Routemaster buses such as this one, still towing a luggage trailer in BEA's 'Speedjack' colours.

←Following the demise of BOAC's Canadair Argonaut ground trainer, retired Comet 4 G-APDT was used for ground training by cabin and engineering trainees and is seen here in May 1974 parked near the perimeter road and BOAC's HQ. It was fitted with engine silencers, so it could still run its engines up.

↓Four months later and Comet 4 G-APDT has been given a pseudo-BA repaint following the merger of BOAC with BEA on 1 April 1974. It is seen in the same location on 8 September 1974. (John Hughes)

➡Another unique, never-to-be-recaptured moment as BOAC Super VC10 G-ASGB sweeps in to land on Runway 28L on 8 August 1974 past the BEA engineering base, both being overdue for rebranding in the BA livery following the BEA/BOAC merger on 1 April 1974.

⬇The Vickers Viscount was probably the most important British airliner and icon at Heathrow for some forty years from the mid-1950s up until the last Viscount flight from Heathrow in April 1996. BEA retained the type into the mid 1970s after the formation of BA, and here we see V802 Viscount G-AOHV at Heathrow on 14 August 1976 with BA Tridents and a TriStar behind. (Richard Hamblin)

←Whilst the Boeing 747s behind retain their BOAC livery, Boeing 707-336C was resplendent in BA's new livery on 31 March 1974 – the day before the new airline was formed! The logo, identity and livery was created by Negus & Negus and presented in 1973. Also part of the identity was a segment of the Union Jack that could be found on the tail fin of the planes. As a result of pressure from BOAC employees, the 'Speedbird' that was part of BOAC's identity was retained and put at the front of the planes.

↓Repainting one fleet of airliners in a new livery is a daunting process, but merging two airlines' fleets and repainting them would take quite some time. As an interim measure, both BEA and BOAC fleets retained their old liveries but with 'British Airways' replacing 'BEA' or 'BOAC'. Here we see former BOAC Boeing 747-136 G-AWNE wearing the hybrid interim scheme on 29 July 1974.

→ The first BA livery was devised by Negus as seen on newly painted Super VC10 G-ASGR, pictured shortly after its arrival on 26 April 1975.

↓ An overview of Terminal 3 and the control tower with the BA fleet of Boeing 707s and a VC10 very much in evidence on 28 March 1976.

➜BA Trident 2E G-AVFE is seen arriving at Terminal 1 on 1 March 1979. This aircraft was initially delivered to BEA in May 1968 and ended up as a fire services training airframe at Belfast Airport in February 1985.

⬇Viewed on approach to Runway 28L on 28 March 1976 are the BA (formerly BOAC) hangars with a pair of VC10s still in BOAC livery.

By now, piston-engined airliners were a rarity and generally only operated by cargo carrier. However, many of the classic first-generation airliners were still in evidence in the 1970s.

The year 1976 was an important one for BA. It took delivery of the first of its seven Concordes and scheduled flights began on 21 January 1976 on the London–Bahrain and Paris–Rio (via Dakar) routes, with BA flights using the 'Speedbird Concorde' callsign to notify air traffic control of the aircraft's unique abilities and restrictions.

↑SABENA, the then state-owned airline of Belgium operated ten Caravelle IVNs, which were also daily visitors to Heathrow from January 1961 until 1977, with some being handed over the airline's charter subsidiary, Sobelair, in 1971. Here we see OO-SRE on 7 March 1973 on push-back prior to departure wearing an experimental reversed-colour 'S'-style tail logo. (W.F. Wilson)

↑Air France initially ordered twelve Caravelle IIIs, and from 6 May 1959 the company commenced a daily service into Heathrow from several airports in France. With their rear-mounted Rolls-Royce Avon turbojets, rear staircase access and unique triangular windows, they soon became very popular with the travelling public and were a daily sight for over twenty years. Here we see F-BHRN, named *Gascogne*, with rear airstairs deployed on 29 January 1973, with a company Boeing 727 alongside. (W.F.Wilson)

→Soviet airline Aeroflot flew its Tupolev Tu-104s into Heathrow on a regular weekly service from Moscow from 1959 up until the late 1960s, when they were replaced by Tupolev Tu-154s. However, they were still occasional visitors in the early 1970s – as seen here, with SSSR-42471 being pushed back on departure by a BEA ground handling crew in June 1973.

↑Vickers VC10 G-ARVG was one of four leased by Gulf Air from BA in 1974, with the first service from Bahrain to London being launched on 1 April 1974. It is seen here on finals to Runway 28L on 8 August 1974 with the BEA engineering base below.

←The entrance to the traffic tunnel in 1974, with a Lufthansa Boeing 737 seen on the runway.

↖Concorde 002, G-BSST, made its first visit to Heathrow on 13 September 1970 and is seen here on its second visit on 1 July 1972. (Stuart Bourne/QAPI)

↑Irish national airline Aer Lingus is another airline that has been part of the Heathrow scene ever since the airport opened to date. Here we see Boeing B737-248 EI-ASD disembarking its passengers after arriving from Dublin on 11 May 1975. (Richard Hamblin)

←As heads of state come and go, Heathrow has seen them all. Here is the personal aircraft of the late Shah of Iran photographed in July 1975. This Boeing 727-81 EP-MRP wears the basic livery of Iran Air and was originally delivered to All Nippon Airways of Japan, before becoming an executive aircraft owned by the Ford Motor Co.

←Considering how new the Airbus family of airliners is, it is hard to believe that the first appearance of an Airbus A300 at Heathrow was over forty years ago! Launch customer Air France commenced services to Heathrow on 23 May 1974 and here we see A300B2 F-BVGB, the sixth production machine, arriving on 26 April 1975.

←The BAC One-Eleven was the most successful airliner since the Vickers Viscount, achieving sales of 231 produced in UK followed by a further licence-built production in Romania. TAROM was operating into Gatwick with Ilyushin IL-18s, which it replaced with its One-Elevens from 1968, switching to Heathrow in the mid-1970s. Whilst most One-Elevens for TAROM were delivered new, Srs.401AK YR-BCG was initially delivered to American Airlines as N5035 in July 1966, being sold to TAROM in July 1972. It is seen here departing Terminal 2 on 22 November 1975. (W.F. Wilson)

↑Iberia Boeing 727-256 EC-CFG is seen with catering being loaded on board prior to departing from Terminal 2 for Palma de Mallorca on 21 March 1976.

↖Another Soviet classic still seen at Heathrow in the 1970s in some numbers, operated by the Eastern Bloc countries, was the Tupolev Tu-134A, of which Czech airline CSA had eleven at the time, including OK-EFK shown here about to depart for Prague on 12 January 1976. (W.F. Wilson/ Author's collection)

↑Iraqi Airways operating into Heathrow with Boeing 707s wearing their smart, distinctive livery. Here is Boeing 707-370C YI-AGE about to depart on 28 May 1976. Fifteen years later, the Gulf War changed things! (W.F. Wilson/Author's collection)

←A historic day occurred on 21 January 1976, as the first British Airways Concorde passenger-carrying service is seen departing Runway 27L for Bahrain in the Persian Gulf. (Stephen Wolf)

←Sikorsky S-61N G-LINK seen at Gatwick on 22 August 1978 after arriving from Heathrow. Airlink was the brand name of a helicopter shuttle service that ran between London's two main airports, Gatwick and Heathrow, from 1978 to 1986. It was operated jointly by British Caledonian Airways and BA Helicopters using a Sikorsky S-61 owned by the BAA. Unfortunately, it was underused and the opening of the M25 motorway killed off its viability. (W.F. Wilson)

↓The death of an Argonaut – but not killed in an adventure with Jason. This was BOAC's last Canadair Argonaut, G-ALHJ, which was used as a ground training airframe for the fire and security services at Heathrow. It lasted until early 1979 when an anti-terrorist training exercise blew off part of the nose, following which it was sadly scrapped.

In 1977, the London Underground Piccadilly Line was extended from Hounslow West via Hatton Cross to Heathrow, connecting the airport with Central London in just under an hour.

Also in 1977, BA and Singapore Airlines shared Concorde for flights between London and Singapore International Airport at Paya Lebar via Bahrain. The aircraft, BA's Concorde G-BOAD, was painted in Singapore Airlines livery on the port side and BA livery on the starboard side. The service was discontinued after only three return flights because of noise complaints from the Malaysian government and could only be reinstated on a new route bypassing Malaysian airspace in 1979. A dispute with India prevented Concorde from reaching supersonic speeds in Indian airspace, so the route was eventually declared not viable and discontinued in 1980.

BEA

FLIGHT GUIDE

INTERNATIONAL ROUTE MAPS

BRITISH EUROPEAN AIRWAYS

Fly the Finest...

FLY TWA
TRANS WORLD AIRLINES

EIGHT

THE 1980S AND MORE EXPANSION

I n 1981, British Airways wanted to drop the 'Airways' part of its title. They were scuppered, however, by British Air Ferries that did the same and both airlines vied with each other for the 'British' titles on their aircraft. BAF claimed that BA couldn't claim 'British' solely for themselves, so BA had a rethink and brought in Landor Associates to introduce a completely new livery comprising a very smart corporate image of grey and dark blue, divided by a red flash and with a silver crown logo on the tail.

Annual passenger numbers had now increased to thirty million and required more terminal space. Terminal 4 was constructed to the south of the southern runway, next to the existing cargo terminal and away from the three older terminals. It was connected to Terminals 1, 2 and 3 by the already-existing Heathrow Cargo Tunnel.

Opened by the Prince and Princess of Wales in April 1986, Terminal 4 became the home for the newly privatised BA. It was connected to Terminals 1, 2 and 3 by the Heathrow Cargo Tunnel. The terminal has an area of 105,481sq.m (1,135,390sq.ft) and is home to the SkyTeam alliance, as well as some unaffiliated carriers. It has recently undergone a £200 milllion upgrade to enable it to accommodate forty-five airlines with an upgraded forecourt to reduce traffic congestion and improve security.

During calibration of Air Traffic Services, it was noticed that there had been a slight magnetic variation to the runways, so on 2 July 1987, Runways 28L & R were repainted as 27L & R to reflect this change

⬆In 1981, BA decided to drop the 'Airways' part of its title, but this was short-lived as they couldn't exclusively trademark the word 'British' as proved by the subsequent adoption of these titles by British Air Ferries. Here we see Trident 2E G-AZXM wearing this livery at Terminal 1 on 26 August 1983. This particular aircraft was formerly 5B-DAA of Cyprus Airways. It ended up being broken up at Southend in February 1985.

➜On December 4 1984, BA revealed a new identity and livery, created by Landor Associates. The new livery featured three colours, which were called pearl grey, midnight blue and brilliant red. Many aspects of the Negus livery were kept. Although the shades were different, the lower part of the fuselage remained blue and the upper part had a slight colour change from white to pearl grey. The part of the Union Jack that was on the lower part of the tail fin was also retained, while the upper part of the tail fin was changed to blue and emblazoned with BA's coat of arms. The font of the name was also changed. The most distinctive change was the addition of the red 'Speedwing', which ran along the entire fuselage. The Speedwing could also be seen in the airline's new logo. Here is Boeing 747-136 G-BBPU in the Landor livery with a BA Lockheed TriStar behind, still in the final Negus livery, on 19 May 1986.

←Two Tridents were painted in BA's 'Landor' livery, Trident 2E G-AVFG depicted here on 20 January 1986 and Trident 3E G-AWZK – but neither flew in these colours, as both were used as cabin and ground handling trainers parked behind the BA hangars. G-AVFG finally went to Heathrow's fire service in September 1990 and got burnt, whilst G-AWZK was adopted by the Trident Preservation Society and eventually got moved to Manchester Airport, where it can be seen today.

←The repainting of the BA fleet into the 'Landor' livery was extended to the ground support vehicles and their coaches looked every bit as smart in this livery as did their aircraft. Here is a BA Leyland Tiger Plaxton Viewmaster IV Express coach seen on a Heathrow–Gatwick shuttle on 6 September 1989.

→An aerial view from the Airlink Sikorsky S-61N in March 1982 showing the BA cargo centre with two Boeing 707s from Air India and BA. (Richard Andrews)

NINE

THE HIGHS AND LOWS OF THE 1990S

On 2 June 1996, Heathrow marked its 50th anniversary with a unique commemorative flypast, the likes of which will never be seen again as it included some of the last of their type in the air. All airport movements were stopped for about fifteen minutes, while a procession of classic aircraft types associated with the airport paraded past. Positioning at Stansted Airport, they consisted of the RAF Battle of Britain Memorial Flight's Lancaster, representing the first Lancastrian flight already mentioned. Then a pair of Dragon Rapides, followed by a Bristol Freighter flanked by a Dove and a Heron, followed by a Douglas DC-4 and DC-6 representing the 'piston era', then representing the 'turboprop era' came a Vickers Viscount, Handley Page Herald and Hawker Siddeley HS748. From the jet age there was the A&AEE Comet 4C, DHL Douglas DC-8-71, AB Airlines BAC One-Eleven 500, Iberia Boeing 727-200, British Midland Boeing 737-300, Singapore Airlines Boeing 747-400, Air Canada Boeing 767, American

→ This statue of Alcock and Brown commemorated their first non-stop transatlantic flight with a Vickers Vimy in 1919. It was originally erected alongside the taxiway at London Airport North. When the Central Area control tower was built, it was moved alongside the tower, as seen here on 13 June 1991. Finally, it currently resides outside the Newall Academy building near the airport entrance on the north side, not far from its original location.

Sculptor William McMillan RA

SIR JOHN ALCOCK AND SIR ARTHUR WHITTEN BROWN
WHO MADE THE FIRST DIRECT FLIGHT ACROSS THE ATLANTIC
ST JOHN'S · NEWFOUNDLAND · CLIFDEN IRELAND
14TH – 15TH JUNE 1919

←↓In September 1990, a 40 per cent scale model of Concorde in BA livery was erected on the roundabout at the entrance to the tunnel, which passes under the northern runway at Heathrow Airport. It was built in four main parts, with an 80ft-long central fuselage section, to which the wings and tail fin were attached. The completed model was placed on the roundabout in September 1990 and was monitored by CCTV and surrounded by an infrared perimeter alarm that was connected to the local Heathrow police station to ensure it was not vandalised.

Airlines McDonnell-Douglas MD-11, BA Boeing 777 and a Virgin Atlantic Airbus A340. The flypast culminated with Concorde flanked by Hawks of the RAF Red Arrows trailing red, white and blue smoke.

In 1997, BA embarked on a rebranding of its entire fleet of aircraft, replacing the trademark Union Jack flag on the tail fin with one of twenty-eight designs created by artists from all over the world, each design representing a country served by BA – although some were not country-focused. Inspired by BA's chief executive, Bob Ayling, the brand was officially unveiled as the 'world tails' image in January 1998. However, these did not prove popular throughout the industry – not helped by Prime Minister Margaret Thatcher draping a cloth over the tail of a model in the new livery, showing her disapproval of the removal of the

Union Flag insignia. Passengers, crew and maintenance staff complained about the schemes, which required individual attention. Heathrow's air traffic controllers, used to recognising airlines by their tail colours, got confused when seeing these aircraft taxying at night with their unfamiliar tails illuminated. Consequently, in 1999 BA abandoned this image, the branding of which had cost them dearly, and reverted to applying the 'Flying Flag' logo to its aircraft, which it still wears at the time of writing.

By April 2001, shortly after Ayling was replaced by Rod Eddington, all of the tail fins were once again painted with the flag, which prevails today at the time of writing.

On 23 June 1998, Heathrow Express started operating a fifteen-minute train service on a newly constructed dedicated line connecting the airport with London's Paddington Station and the Great Western Main Line.

↑On 2 June 1996, Heathrow Airport marked its 50th anniversary with a flypast of representative airliner types that have served the airport over the years. This culminated in a formation flypast by Concorde with Hawks of the RAF Red Arrows aerobatic team.

In 1997, BA really stirred things up with their ethnic world tails designs. Also known as the utopia or world image tail fins, they used art and designs from international artists and other sources to represent countries on BA's route network. The signature of the artist was carried near the design on the tail. People either loved them or hated them. Prime Minister Margaret Thatcher detested them and was seen to cover the tail of a model with her handkerchief; the CEO of BA subsequently lost his job. They dumped the classy Landor livery, and perhaps the biggest flaw in the world tails effort was that it was a marked a step away from BA's corporate image, not to mention the explicitly British image the company had strenuously emphasised over the previous decade. But BA forged ahead with world tails as a sort of global outreach, in order to solidify its position as the undisputed market leader in world travel. Not surprisingly, wiping the Union Jack flag from its tails sent the subliminal message that being British was bad for business, which created a consumer backlash at home. Eventually, in 2001, BA abandoned the world tails entirely and repainted them all in a stylised Union Jack, known as Chatham Dockyard, which prevails today. Here we see Boeing 747-436, wearing the Africa world tail image on 10 July 1999, with another 747 behind in the old Landor scheme.

TEN

FAREWELL TO THE VISCOUNT

Vickers Viscounts, with the distinctive whistling sound of their Rolls-Royce Dart turboprop engines, were iconic airliners at London Heathrow for over forty years. The Viscount was a tremendous success for Vickers and the British aircraft industry, with no less than 445 being built and serving with airlines worldwide. If the type's range was within London's Heathrow Airport, then that is where they would be seen. The first production aircraft, Series 701 G-ALWE, was delivered to BEA at London Airport on 3 March 1953. This heralded the start of a long association with the Viscount for BEA, which went on to order and operate a total of eighty-eight Viscounts of all variants. When BEA and BOAC merged to form BA on 1 April 1974, the resulting airline continued to operate Viscounts, some of which had been inherited from Cambrian Airways and Northeast (ex-BKS) Airlines.

When the Viscounts were finally retired by BA in May 1982, several were sold to smaller airlines including British Air Ferries, which was renamed British World Airlines. The Viscount had played such a big part in the history of BEA, BA and the London Airport scene for over forty years that a special ceremony and flight was arranged for the last passenger Viscount flight from London Heathrow, which took place on April 18 1996. After years of plane spotting from the airport roof gardens, dreaming of having a flight in a Viscount, the author was delighted when British World Airlines invited him to be one of the VIP passengers on this flight. The aircraft selected for this flight was due to be G-AOHM, but due to a ground handling accident at Stansted this had to be switched to G-APEY,

↑18 April 1996 marked the last flight of a Vickers Viscount from Heathrow. The type has been the most important and prolific type in the airport's history. The last flight was carried out by V.806 G-APEY of British World Airlines and which first joined BEA in July 1958 and flew BA's last turboprop flight Jersey–Heathrow on 28 March 1981 before being sold to British Air Ferries (later British World Airlines) the following month. This photograph shows it departing Heathrow on its last day, 18 April 1996, passing a BA Concorde and Boeing 747.

which was specially flown down from Glasgow for the ceremonial flight. This particular Viscount not only turned out to be the very last airworthy passenger Viscount in the UK but also to be the same plane the author saw in BEA colours on his very first spotting trip on 7 August 1961, as recorded in his spotting logbook. It had only taken the author thirty-five years to get a flight on a Viscount and just in time since this was the very last one to be operated from Heathrow!

On that day, he was very privileged to share the event with Sir George Edwards, the Viscount's designer, Lord King, then chairman of BA and Sir Peter Masefield, chairman of BEA during the Viscount years and chairman of the BAA 1965–71. Alas, all three are no longer with us.

➜ Three VIP guests that were on board the last Viscount flight on 18 April 1996 were: Sir Peter Masefield (chairman of BEA during the Viscount years), Sir George Edwards (the Viscount's designer) and Lord John King (then chairman of BA).

↑On board Viscount G-APEY during its last flight from Heathrow, champagne is served to the guest passengers.

↓At the helm of Viscount G-APEY en route to Stansted during its last flight from Heathrow is British World's Captain Colin Towle.

↑Passenger heaven! It was the propeller's turning and quiet hum of the Rolls-Royce Dart turboprops, viewed from one of the large oval passenger windows, that made the Viscount so popular throughout its career. One last chance to savour this view during the last flight.

ELEVEN

VIEWING FACILITIES

Even in the early days, car parking charges for the day were high in the dedicated airport car parks, so we used to park the car by the pub on the Bath Road and walk through the traffic tunnel that connects the north side with the Central Area and runs beneath the main runway.

Travel by air was still expensive for the average person and it would be another decade before I took my first flight out of Heathrow. The viewing terraces were packed during the summer months as enthusiasts, families and plane spotters alike enjoyed a day out watching the comings and goings of the world's airlines. There were shops, a cafeteria, a children's play area and even a paddling pool for those too young to appreciate what they were seeing. In fact everything was done to promote air travel in the UK – a far cry from today, where plane spotters and the like are not welcome, no facilities are provided and security against terrorist threats dominates!

Viewing and photographic facilities at Heathrow were excellent for the aviation enthusiast. The days of London Airport North in the early 1950s, where the aircraft taxied right past you, were followed by the wonderful viewing terraces in the Central Area, which lasted from the mid 1950s right up until 2001, when the last viewing terrace was closed on advice from the government, following the 9/11 attack in New York in 2001 and the 7/7 bombings in London in 2005. The most revered location for plane spotters, the terminal building roof terraces, were reduced to a single balcony by 1998 until their demise.

↑Like father, like son. The author believes that introducing children to a hobby and sharing interests has always been an important part of a stable upbringing. Many parents brought their children to Heathrow's viewing terraces for them to enjoy the experience. Furthermore, it was a nice achievement to recreate the scene shown earlier on the spectators' viewing terraces before they closed, showing that you could still get close to the aircraft in the 1980s. Aged 5, the author's son, Richard, is depicted clutching his binoculars with an Iberia Douglas DC-9 behind on 1 June 1985.

←One of the last operators of the Vickers Viscount into Heathrow was British Midland Airways. G-BMAT seen here with a company DC-9 behind is depicted in March 1985. It was originally delivered to South African Airways as ZS-CDW until being sold to BMA in January 1972 as G-AZLT. On 6 October 1980, it crashed at Leeds/Bradford Airport, aquaplaning on the wet runway which it overran. It was subsequently repaired and re-registered as G-BMAT on 30 March 1981 and returned to service.

←Belgian national airline SABENA existed from 1923 to 2001, when it filed for bankruptcy. It had been a regular part of the Heathrow scene since it opened in 1946, upgrading its aircraft as the years went by. Here we see Boeing 737-229 OO-SDL on 1 June 1985 in company with a Lufthansa Boeing 737 and a Swissair Airbus A310.

↑Another classic airline that had been seen at Heathrow for many years was Olympic Airways of Greece. Here is SX-BEI, an Airbus A300-600, viewed from the last spectators' viewing terrace on 13 July 1997.

→One of the last bastions for plane spotters and spectators was on the roof of Terminal 3's car park. This is the unfriendly notice that greets anyone that attempts this today! (Richard Vandervord)

Viewing strictly prohibited Please leave the area immediately

Security was stepped up and perimeter fences reinforced. Passengers had to endure more severe security measures and the free and easy atmosphere of the airport changed. The airport felt it no longer needed to promote itself or air travel and plane spotters were not made welcome. After that, the Heathrow visitor's centre was opened on what was London Airport North adjacent to the main runway. Even if they were using that runway, it was woefully inadequate for viewing, and especially for photography, as it was across a road, behind a high fence and faced the sun. Because of this, visitor numbers fell and the centre finally closed in March 2010. After that, there was nowhere for plane spotters to go and photograph the airliners, apart from the end of the runway in use at the time, outside the fence. If the authorities invested a little money on opening a dedicated spectators' viewing area, it would pay dividends for them! A few airports around the world have started doing this and it has reaped benefits all round.

The top of Terminal 3's car park used to be another favourite viewing area, but go there today and you are greeted with an unfriendly sign that reads 'Viewing is strictly prohibited – please leave the area immediately' reinforced by CCTV cameras should anyone linger there.

With the rooftop viewing areas now closed, nostalgic enthusiasts could only admire the iconic buildings in the Central Area – the ATC tower and terminal buildings from below and remember their childhood spotting days. Alas, a new ATC tower was being constructed out in the middle of the airport, and the days for the old tower were numbered, although it was rumoured that when it finally closed, it would be retained for storage and as a library. The tower closed in 2007 and air traffic operations moved to the new tower, which was out in the middle of the airport and twice as high as the old tower, giving 360-degree views of the entire airport. Hopes that the 1950s ATC tower would be made a listed building and not be demolished were dashed when the bulldozers moved in and it was very

←A last look at the old iconic ATC tower from the Underground station entrance in July 2008.

←A sad moment caught by the author on 9 January 2013 from St George's Chapel, as the iconic Heathrow control tower is demolished, having housed controllers that have safely looked after thousands of planes and their passengers since it opened in 1955.

↑Designed by architect Sir Frederick Gibberd, the old control tower closed in 2012 after almost sixty years' service. It had been used as offices for the last five years of its life, after air traffic control moved to the new control tower in 2007.

sadly and unceremoniously demolished in January 2013. With a heavy nostalgic heart, the author returned once more, to watch the much-loved iconic tower 'die'; It had presided over so many arrivals and departures for nearly fifty years, not to mention all the aviation enthusiasts that have seen it.

As if that was not enough, in 2010, work had already begun on demolishing the Queen's Building and Terminal 2 to make way for a brand-new terminal building, which was opened in June 2014.

Today's Heathrow is almost unrecognisable from its early beginnings of the 1940s, through the construction on the Central Terminal Area in the 1950s to the ever expanding airport, including the construction of a new BA freight terminal in the early 1970s. Terminal 4 was formally inaugurated by the Prince and Princess of Wales on 1 April 1986, followed by the privatisation of Heathrow Airport by the BAA on 1 August 1986. Finally, Terminal 5 was constructed in 2007 between the northern and southern runways at the west end of the Heathrow site and was opened

←As EU noise and pollution restrictions came into force, so the old Russian-built airliners became rarer and rarer, the last operator of the Tupolev Tu-154 into Heathrow being Pulkovo Airlines. Here is RA85832 seen on finals to Runway 27R on 7 May 2005 during one of its last visits.

by Queen Elizabeth II on 14 March 2008, some nineteen years after its inception. It opened to the public on 27 March 2008.

The propeller-powered airliners are now all but a memory at Heathrow, as are the first-generation jets. The first Boeing 747 arrived in 1970, when Pan Am's first scheduled 747 touched down on 12 January 1970. Consequently this spawned a new generation of wide-bodied airliners with Airbus and Boeing competing for sales; both companies still dominate the Heathrow airliner scene today. That same year, however, Concorde touched down at Heathrow for the first time, giving passengers a choice between cheap but slow transatlantic travel and supersonic but very expensive crossings. In the end, it was the former that prevailed.

The variety of sounds and sights that were cherished by plane spotters in the 1950s,'60s and '70s have gone. They have been replaced with types that all sound and look very similar. Noise abatement, anti-pollution, capacity and economy of fuel have all played a role in shaping the airliners of today, ousting the charismatic but anti-social last of the old-generation jets, such as the BAC One-Eleven 8 and Russian Tu-134 and Tu-154. The last of these was Concorde, which was finally withdrawn in November 2003.

↑A sad day for may aircraft enthusiasts: 24 October 2003 was a Heathrow milestone: BA withdrew its Concordes from service, bringing to a close the world's only supersonic passenger service. The final scheduled commercial flight was BA002 from JFK operated by G-BOAG. BA's fleet of seven aircraft was subsequently dispersed for preservation at Barbados (AE), Edinburgh (AA), Filton (AF), Manchester (AC), New York (AD) and Seattle (AG) with one (AB) remaining at Heathrow. Here we see three of the Concordes, G-BOAE,'F and 'G all parked together outside the BA hangar on 8 November 2003 following withdrawal. (John Hughes)

TWELVE

THE 2000S – BIGGER AND BETTER

Noise and pollution have been dramatically reduced at Heathrow in recent years. On 1 April 2002, Chapter 2 of the EU's noise regulations policy came into force, which banned noisy first-generation jets such as the Boeing 707 and 727, as well as the early Soviet jet airliners. 'Hush kits' were fitted to the engines on some types, such as the BAC One-Eleven, which alleviated the problem to some extent, and today's airliners are 85 per cent quieter than those early jets.

Alas, Concorde fell under this new legislation and on 10 April 2003, Air France and BA simultaneously announced that they would retire Concorde later that year. They cited low passenger numbers following the 25 July 2000 crash, the slump in air travel following the 11 September 2001 attacks and rising maintenance costs. Although Concorde was technologically advanced when introduced in the 1970s, thirty years later, its analogue cockpit was dated. There had been little commercial pressure to upgrade Concorde due to a lack of competing aircraft, unlike other airliners of the same era such as the Boeing 747. By its retirement, it was the last aircraft in BA's fleet that had a flight engineer; other aircraft, such as the modernised 747-400, had eliminated the role. The day of the 26 November 2003 was a sad day for aircraft enthusiasts, when the last Concorde flight took off from Heathrow, as G-BOAF was retired to its birthplace of Filton, Bristol, where it resides today. In the end Concorde was running at a loss for BA, the public not wishing to pay a premium for supersonic travel as the slower, more economical 'jumbos' prevailed.

← Wearing BA's Landor livery, Concorde G-BOAE retracts its undercarriage as it lifts off from Runway 27L en route to New York on 8 May 1994.

Today, the Heathrow scene is dominated by fuel-efficient Airbus and Boeing airliners, a far cry from the variety of sights and sounds generated by the multitude of piston, turboprop and early jets of the 1950s and '60s.

By the time Heathrow celebrated its 60th anniversary in 2006 it had handled around 1.4 billion passengers on over 14 million flights. BAA plc was bought in 2006 by a consortium led by Ferrovial, a Spanish firm specialising in the design, construction, financing, operation and maintenance of transport, urban and services infrastructure. In March 2009 the company was required to sell Gatwick and Stansted airports, and over the following years sold all its airports other than Heathrow. The company was renamed Heathrow Airport Holdings in 2012 to reflect its main business.

In 2006, the new £105 million Pier 6 was completed at Terminal 3 in order to accommodate the Airbus A380, providing four new aircraft stands. Other alterations were carried out across the airport, totalling in excess of £340 million, in readiness for the Airbus A380. The first test flight into Heathrow took place on 18 May 2006, but following production delays scheduled services did not commence from Heathrow until 18 March 2008, when Singapore Airlines A380 registered 9V-SKA touched down from Singapore with 470 passengers on board, marking the first ever European commercial flight by the Airbus A380.

Redevelopment of Terminal 3's forecourt through the addition of a new four-lane drop-off area and a large pedestrianised plaza, complete with canopy to the front of the terminal building, was completed in 2007. These improvements were intended to enhance passengers' experiences, reduce traffic congestion and improve security. As part of this project, Virgin Atlantic was assigned its own dedicated check-in area, known as Zone A, which features a large sculpture and atrium.

→ The Concorde model at the entrance to Heathrow, repainted in the final BA 'flying flag' livery, as seen on 15 June 1997. When the lease for this prime advertising spot was due for renewal in early 2007 the cost had risen to over £1.5 million per year. BA did not feel that another six-year deal suited their marketing requirements – especially with their move to the new Terminal 5 due imminently. They could also not justify keeping a model of an aircraft that they no longer flew. Ultimately this meant that a decision had to be made as to what to do with G-CONC. BA had two options available to them: donate it to a museum, or scrap it. It now resides with the Brooklands Museum, who have fully restored it.

↑Another never-to-be-repeated moment: Singapore Airlines Airbus A380 9V-SKB lifts off from Runway 27L, with the old control tower visible in the distance, on 20 July 2009. Launch customer Singapore Airlines were the first airline to operate the giant A380 into Heathrow direct from Changi on 18 March 2008, following delivery of their third aircraft.

In March 2007, the scale model of Concorde that had been pride of place at Heathrow Airport's entrance for sixteen years, was removed. BA decided not to renew the £1.5 million annual rent to advertise on the roundabout at the gateway to the airport. More than 25 million travellers a year passed by the 4:10 scale model of the supersonic airliner. The old BA model was donated to Brooklands Museum, Weybridge in Surrey, where it can be seen today.

⬇Security and breakdown vehicles on standby near the tunnel entrance in a case of any accidents or incidents.

←The one-third scale 45-ton model of an Emirates Airbus A380 that has stood on the roundabout before the airport's tunnel entrance since July 2008, when it replaced the model of Concorde.

The following year the Concorde model was replaced by a giant model of an Emirates Airbus A380 in an unveiling ceremony on 23 July 2008. The completion of the giant A380 replica was the culmination of an ambitious eighteen-month project to place the Dubai-based carrier at the gateway to the world's busiest international airport, and at one of the most prestigious advertising sites in the UK. Tim Clark, the airline's president, said:

> The gateway to the world's busiest international airport is a fitting home for Emirates. We expect this landmark site to become an icon for both Heathrow and Emirates. While the previous Concorde model represented

the past, our A380 represents the future – and it is a future of cleaner, quieter aircraft.

The one-third-scale model was flown in ten component parts to Heathrow on 5 July 2008. Since then, specialist teams worked around the clock to launch Emirates' 'first' A380. The replica was built by US-based Penwal at its manufacturing base in California over a six-month period, using plans provided by the A380's manufacturer Airbus in Toulouse. It was then transported by giant truck to Ontario Airport in Los Angeles where it was flown to Heathrow aboard a massive Antonov An-124 cargo plane, organised by the Emirates SkyCargo team. A special mechanical ramp was flown into London from Germany to offload the plane, as it was too heavy for the Antonov's winch crane. The wing section of the plane required a police escort as it was driven from Heathrow to the roundabout site.

The world's leading aviation museum, the Smithsonian Air and Space Museum in Washington DC, has stated it is the largest known aircraft model in existence. A world record submission is currently with Guinness World Records. Model quick facts include:

Weighs more than 45 tonnes
Wingspan of 26 metres and a length of 24 metres
Same size as a real Boeing 737
Exact 1:3 scale of the real A380, the world's largest airliner
More than twice the size of the roundabout's previous Concorde model
Made of glass-reinforced plastic over a steel frame
Foundations required 600 tonnes of concrete.

→Heading out of the traffic tunnel underpass, the Emirates Airbus A380 model comes into view.

On 1 December 2008, Emirates launched its first Airbus A380 service to London and it is currently the largest operator of the type into Heathrow. It was not the first airline to operate the huge giant into Heathrow; Singapore Airlines became the first airline to operate the Airbus A380 on 25 October 2007. With the delivery of the third A380, services to London Heathrow commenced on 18 March 2008.

Terminal 5, located between the northern and southern runways at the west end of the Heathrow site, was opened by Her Majesty the Queen on 14 March 2008. It was opened to the public on 27 March 2008, with BA and its partner company Iberia having exclusive use of this terminal. During the two weeks after its opening, operations were disrupted by problems with the terminal's IT systems. Coupled with insufficient testing and staff training, this caused over 500 flights to be cancelled. Until March 2012, Terminal 5 was exclusively used by BA as its global hub; however, because of the merger, on 25 March Iberia's operations at Heathrow were moved to the terminal, making it the home of International Airlines Group.

Built at a cost of £4.3 billion, the new terminal consists of a four-storey main terminal building (Concourse A) with an area of 300,000sq.m (3,200,000sq.ft) and two satellite buildings linked to the main terminal by an underground people-mover transit system. Concourse B covers 60,000sq.m (650,000sq.ft). It has sixty aircraft stands and capacity for 30 million passengers annually as well as more than 100 shops and restaurants. The second satellite (Concourse C) includes dedicated aircraft stands for the Airbus A380 and became fully operational on 1 June 2011.

The transport network around the airport has been extended to cope with the increase in passenger numbers. A dedicated motorway spur links the M25 between junctions 14 and 15 to the terminal, which includes a 3,800-space multi-storey car park. A more distant long-stay car park for business passengers is connected to the terminal by a personal rapid transit system, which became operational in spring 2011.

In 2010, work commenced to demolish the old Terminal 2, another iconic building, so sacred to many aviation enthusiasts for four decades, from the mid 1950s onwards, for its rooftop viewing facilities This was to make way for its £1 billion replacement, which opened on 4 June 2014

British Midland Airways, whose head office was at Donington Hall in Castle Donington, close to East Midlands Airport, flew to destinations in Europe, the Middle East, Africa, North America and Central Asia from its operational base at London Heathrow Airport. At its peak it held

↑Terminal 3 is home to Virgin Atlantic. This view from the tower includes examples of their Boeing 747, Airbus A330 and A340 fleets, seen on 19 June 2013. (Richard Vandervord)

↑A last look at the Queen's Building on 22 July 2008, before its demolition began.

↑The old Terminal 2 with a new frontage photographed in July 2008 with an artist's impression showing what the new Terminal 2 will look like.

*c.*13 per cent of all take-off and landing slots and operated over 2,000 flights a week. BMI was a member of Star Alliance from 1 July 2000 until 20 April 2012.

On 20 April 2012, BMI was acquired from Lufthansa by International Airlines Group (IAG) and was integrated into BA by 27 October 2012. Consequently another well-known airline name disappeared from the Heathrow scene, one that had operated from there since the early 1970s.

On 30 April 2012, the first Boeing 787 Dreamliner landed at London's Heathrow Airport, and aircraft number N787BX was formally welcomed into one of BA's gargantuan hangars at the eastern end of the airfield, prior to delivery of the first for BA. This event also marked the official reopening of the former BOAC hangar following its conversion to handle all the aircraft types in BA's future fleet programme, including the Airbus A380.

The hangar, built in the 1950s and now Grade II listed by English Heritage, features unsupported internal arches specially designed by the late Sir Evan Owen Williams. The conversion required the preservation

↑Inside the old Terminal 2 showing the Departures Hall in July 2008. The original Terminal 2 opened as the Europa Building in 1955 and building was the airport's oldest terminal. It had an area of 49,654sq.m (534,470sq.ft) and was designed to handle around 1.2 million passengers annually. In its final years it accommodated up to 8 million. A total of 316 million passengers passed through the terminal in its lifetime. The building was demolished in 2010, along with the Queen's Building.

➜Grave of the old control tower! June 2013 and the old tower has gone, whilst the new Terminal 2 is almost complete. (Richard Vandervord)

of the graceful internal arches, but also necessitated the lifting in to place of a 24-ton 'eyebrow' that effectively forms a notch in the beam above the entrance doors and that allows the tallest tail fins to pass through unhindered.

During 2012, demolition of the old Terminals 1 and 2 was completed, followed by the ATC tower in January 2013, which had been an icon at Heathrow for fifty-seven years. It was replaced by a 87m (285ft) ATC tower, costing £50 million, located in the middle of the airfield, which was officially opened on 13 June 2007 by the secretary of state for Transport, Douglas Alexander. The new £1 billion replacement Terminal 2 opened on 4 June 2014.

Today, Heathrow is the world's busiest international airport and the hub of the civil aviation world. Over 67 million passengers travel through the airport annually on services offered by ninety airlines travelling to over 180 destinations in over ninety countries. The airport is owned and operated by Heathrow Airport Holdings, which itself is owned by FGP Topco Ltd, an international consortium led by the Spanish Ferrovial Group that includes Caisse de dépôt et placement du Québec and Government of Singapore Investment Corporation. Heathrow is the primary hub for BA and the primary operating base for Virgin Atlantic.

In September 2012, the British government established the Airports Commission, an independent commission chaired by Sir Howard Davies to review various options for increasing capacity at UK airports. The commission shortlisted two options for expanding Heathrow in its interim report in 2013, along with a third option for expanding Gatwick Airport. The final report, published on 1 July 2015, backed a third runway at Heathrow.

The airport has altered beyond recognition since its earliest years when the first flights used temporary tents for arrivals and departures. Today, the airport has five terminals, a brand-new control tower and plans for further

➜Opened in 2007, Heathrow's new control tower stands 87m tall, twice as high as the old tower and the highest in the UK. (NATS photograph)

expansion. Heathrow plans to spent £600 million each year between 2014 and 2019 for upgrading operations, yet potential plans to build a third runway are hotly contested, despite the airport almost operating at full capacity. Heathrow is one of the busiest airports in the world, seeing on average 191,200 passengers arriving and departing every day. Additionally, it is host to eighty-four airlines and serves 184 destinations. Although thought of as a place of transition by many, it also directly

↓Costing £50 million to construct, the new control tower gives controllers an excellent 360-degree panoramic view. (NATS photograph)

↑One of the views from the control tower looking north-east towards runway 27R/O9L and Terminal 1 North, which host mainly Airbuses from BA and Aer Lingus. (Richard Vandervord)

↑Looking due east from the control tower, this is Terminal 3 with airliners from Air Canada, EgyptAir and Virgin Atlantic in view. (Richard Vandervord)

↑As a BA Airbus A320 touches down on Runway 09L, we see a pair of QANTAS Airbus A380s alongside the bulk fuel storage tanks. (Richard Vandervord)

←Cranes are busy as the new Terminal 2 takes shape on 9 January 2013.

→The airport's newest terminal, officially known as the Queen's Terminal, was opened on 4 June 2014. Designed by Spanish architect Luis Vidal, it was built on the site previously occupied by the original Terminal 2 and the Queen's Building. The main complex was completed in November 2013 and underwent six months of testing before opening to passengers. It includes a satellite pier (T2B), a 1,340-space car park, an energy centre and a cooling station to generate chilled water. There are fifty-two shops and seventeen bars and restaurants.

↓St George's Chapel remained in situ throughout the reconstruction of the Central Area. Here Terminal 2 is depicted from the area outside the chapel.

→ Terminal 3 today.

↓ The new Terminal 2, the Queen's Terminal.

⬆The Central Bus Station with the new Terminal 2 behind.

⬅RIP old control tower; this is where it once stood, now a car park.

employs some 45,000 people, which will continue to grow with the recent and future developments.

The airport's latest terminal, officially known as the Queen's Terminal, was opened on 4 June 2014, with Terminal 1 closing the following year. Designed by Spanish architect Luis Vidal, the new Terminal 2 was built on the site previously occupied by the original Terminal 2 and the Queen's Building. The main complex was completed in November 2013

and underwent six months of testing before opening to passengers. It includes a satellite pier (T2B), a 1,340-space car park, an energy centre and a cooling station to generate chilled water. There are fifty-two shops and seventeen bars and restaurants. Inside the building, passengers are greeted by a gigantic metal suspended sculpture called *Slipstream*, which was created by Richard Wilson and is over 70m (230ft) long and weighs 77 tons.

↖The new Terminal 2 departures entrance.

↑Airline ticket desks in Terminal 2.

←A huge bank of check-in desks greet departing passengers in Terminal 2.

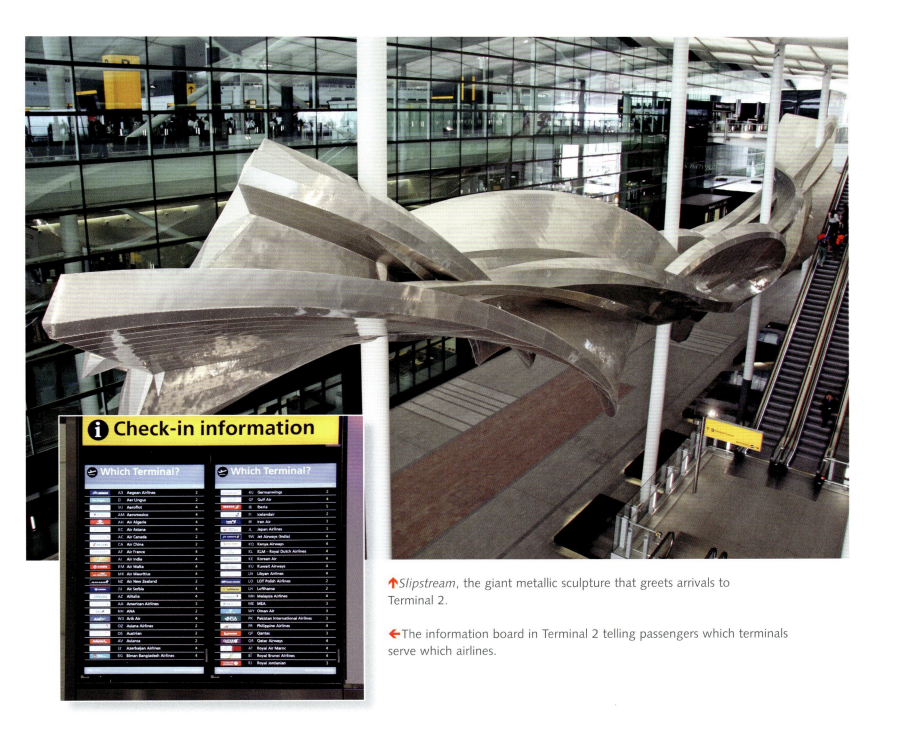

↑*Slipstream*, the giant metallic sculpture that greets arrivals to Terminal 2.

←The information board in Terminal 2 telling passengers which terminals serve which airlines.

ℹ Check-in information

✈ Which Terminal?

A3	Aegean Airlines	2
EI	Aer Lingus	2
SU	Aeroflot	4
AM	Aeromexico	4
AH	Air Algerie	4
KC	Air Astana	4
AC	Air Canada	2
CA	Air China	2
AF	Air France	4
AI	Air India	4
KM	Air Malta	4
MK	Air Mauritius	4
NZ	Air New Zealand	2
JU	Air Serbia	4
AZ	Alitalia	4
AA	American Airlines	3
NH	ANA	2
W3	Arik Air	4
OZ	Asiana Airlines	2
OS	Austrian	2
AV	Avianca	2
J2	Azerbaijan Airlines	3
BG	Biman Bangladesh Airlines	4

✈ Which Terminal?

4U	Germanwings	2
GF	Gulf Air	4
IB	Iberia	5
FI	Icelandair	2
IR	Iran Air	3
JL	Japan Airlines	3
9W	Jet Airways (India)	4
KQ	Kenya Airways	4
KL	KLM – Royal Dutch Airlines	4
KE	Korean Air	4
KU	Kuwait Airways	4
LN	Libyan Airlines	4
LO	LOT Polish Airlines	2
LH	Lufthansa	2
MH	Malaysia Airlines	4
ME	MEA	3
WY	Oman Air	3
PK	Pakistan International Airlines	3
PR	Philippine Airlines	4
QF	Qantas	3
QR	Qatar Airways	4
AT	Royal Air Maroc	4
BI	Royal Brunei Airlines	4
RJ	Royal Jordanian	3

The new Terminal 2 is used by Star Alliance members that fly from Heathrow (consolidating the airlines under Star Alliance's co-location policy 'move under one roof') with the exception of Air India, which uses Terminal 4. Aer Lingus, Little Red (Virgin Atlantic's domestic operation), Germanwings and Icelandair also operate from the terminal. The airlines moved from their original locations over a six-month period, with only 10 per cent of flights operating in the first six weeks (United Airlines' transatlantic flights) to avoid the opening problems seen at Terminal 5. Development will continue at the terminal to increase capacity in preparation for the closure of Terminal 3 in 2019.

Car parking in the airport car parks has always been expensive. In the 1960s, the author's father and son always parked our car outside the Three Magpies pub on the Bath Road, as car parking there was free. We would then walk through the airport's tunnel to the terminal buildings. The origin of the Three Magpies is over 150 years old and it is the last public house on the Bath Road. Located beside the main entrance to Heathrow Airport,

it has witnessed all the changes described in this book from being the local pub in the hamlet of Heathrow, through to the opening in 1946, and on to today's sprawling metropolis. Amazingly, the Three Magpies still exists today as a thriving pub – and even more amazingly they still have free car parking outside the pub! However, pedestrians are no longer permitted to walk through the tunnel

With future expansion still on the cards for Heathrow, who knows what will transpire? Singapore Airlines inaugurated the first Airbus A380 service to London in 2008, increasing passenger capacity and consequently passenger-handling capacity requirements – which begs the question, how much more can Heathrow expand in the future? The aspiration of installing a third runway remains to be realised.

➜ One building that has witnessed all the changes to Heathrow and is still standing for business is the Three Magpies public house, which is over 150 years old and the last public house on the A4 Bath Road outside the main airport entrance.

Beating the traffic: Ian Haskell got special permission to overfly Heathrow Airport very early on the morning of 25 June 2014, four days after the longest day, to take the following aerial views.

↑The new Terminal 2 and annex.

↑The British Airways engineering base.

↑The BA engineering base with mainly Boeing 777s outside and the preserved Concorde G-BOAB visible.

➜Wave, please! The 87m-high control tower from the air.

↖Looking due west down Runway 27L. This view gives a good overall perspective of the airport.

↑Terminal 2, with the Central Bus Station and car park where the original control tower stood in the foreground.

←Terminal 5, exclusively used by BA.

↑A very busy Terminal 5, looking north along the lines of BA aircraft, mainly dominated by Boeing 747s, 777s and 737s.

↖An overall view looking north-east with Terminal 4 in the top-right of the photograph. (Richard Vandervord)

↑An overall view looking south-east with Terminal 5 in the foreground. (Richard Vandervord)

←Terminal 5 looking north along the lines of BA aircraft, mainly dominated by Boeing 747s, 777s and 737s. (Richard Vandervord)

THIRTEEN

75TH ANNIVERSARY HIGHS AND LOWS

I n 2019, British Airways celebrated the 100th anniversary of its founder roots, which started in 1919 with a de Havilland DH.4A of Air Transport and Travel Ltd, which operated to Paris from Hounslow Heath, very near to the current Heathrow. To mark this centenary milestone, four of its aircraft were repainted in the airline's retro colours. Airbus A319, G-EUPJ was repainted in BEA's 'red square' livery of the 1960s, Boeing 747-436, G-BYGC, was repainted in the original 1971 BOAC delivery scheme, Boeing 747-436, G-CIVB, was repainted in the first British Airways 'Negus' livery of the 1970s and Boeing 747-436, G-CIVL was repainted in British Airways 'Landor' livery of the 1980s.

The following year, the airline and Heathrow Airport as a whole faced its worst nightmare as Covid-19, the pandemic virus, spread from China across the world and decimated air travel for all. This resulted in airlines collapsing and those who remained struggling to survive by utilising their empty passenger space with freight. British Airways put the majority of its fleet into store and was forced to prematurely retire its entire Boeing 747 'Jumbo' fleet, which were flown out to Kemble (Cotswold Airport) and St Athan (Cardiff) to await their fate. The last two departed London Heathrow on 8 October 2020, marking the end of an era. British Airways had operated 103 examples of the Boeing 747 from Heathrow and at its height it was the world's biggest operator of the 400 series with a fleet of 57.

↑British Airways Boeing 747-436, G-BYGC, repainted in the original early 1970s BOAC livery commemorating the airline's centenary, seen landing at Heathrow on 4 March 2019.

←British Airways Airbus A319-131, G-EUPJ, repainted in the 1960s livery of BEA (British European Airways) seen here on 16 March 2019.

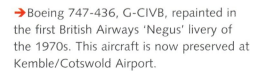

→Boeing 747-436, G-CIVB, repainted in the first British Airways 'Negus' livery of the 1970s. This aircraft is now preserved at Kemble/Cotswold Airport.

←Boeing 747-436, G-CIVL, repainted in the 1985 British Airways 'Landor' livery.

'Out to grass' - the sad sight of British Airways Boeing 747s withdrawn from use at Kemble in October 2020 (Author's photos)